A Hacker's Guide

to

Project Management

Second Edition

A Hacker's Guide

to

Project Management

Second Edition

Andrew K. Johnston

Illustrated by Sarah Ward, Helen Floate and Andrew K. Johnston

OXFORD AMSTERDAM BOSTON LONDON NEW YORK PARIS
SAN DIEGO SAN FRANCISCO SINGAPORE SYDNEY TOKYO

Butterworth-Heinemann
An imprint of Elsevier Science
Linacre House, Jordan Hill, Oxford OX2 8DP
200 Wheeler Road, Burlington MA 01803

First published 1995
Reprinted 1996, 1997, 1998, 1999, 2000, 2001
Second edition 2003

British Library Cataloguing in Publication Data
A catalogue record for this book is available from the British Library

Library of Congress Cataloguing in Publication Data
A catalogue record for this book is available from the Library of Congress

ISBN: 0750657464

For information on all Butterworth-Heinemann publications visit our website at
www.bh.com

Written and typeset by the author, using Microsoft Word-for-Windows. The Gantt
and PERT charts on page 80 were prepared using Microsoft Project.

Printed and bound in Great Britain

Computer Weekly Professional Series

There are few professions which require as much continuous updating as that of the IS executive. Not only does the hardware and software scene change relentlessly, but also ideas about the actual management of the IS function are being continuously modified, updated and changed. Thus keeping abreast of what is going on is really a major task.

The Butterworth-Heinemann – *Computer Weekly* Professional Series has been created to assist IS executives keep up to date with the management ideas and issues of which they need to be aware.

One of the key objectives of the series is to reduce the time it takes for leading edge management ideas to move from the academic and consulting environments into the hands of the IT practitioner. Thus this series employs appropriate technology to speed up the publishing process. Where appropriate some books are supported by CD-ROM or by additional information or templates located on the Web.

This series provides IT professionals with an opportunity to build up a bookcase of easily accessible, but detailed information on the important issues that they need to be aware of to successfully perform their jobs as they move into the new millennium.

Aspiring or already established authors are invited to get in touch with me directly if they would like to be published in this series.

Dr Dan Remenyi
Series Editor
Dan.remenyi@mcil.co.uk

Other titles in the Series
IT investment – making a business case
The effective measurement and management of IT costs and benefits
Stop IT project failures through risk management
Understanding the Internet
Prince 2: a practical handbook
Considering computer contracting?
David Taylor's Inside Track
Corporate politics for IT managers: how to get streetwise
Subnet design for efficient networks
Information warfare: corporate attack and defence in a digital world
Delivering IT and e-business value
Reinventing the IT department
The project manager's toolkit

Contents

Introduction

Managing a software development project is a complex process. There are lots of deliverables to produce, standards and procedures to observe, plans and budgets to meet, and different people to manage or report to. Project management doesn't just start and end with designing and building the system. Once you've specified, designed and built (or bought) the system it still needs to be properly tested, documented and settled into the live environment. This can seem like a maze to the inexperienced project manager, or even to the experienced project manager unused to a particular environment.

Like all mazes, it's much easier if you have a guide. Let this book help you find your way around. I can't promise that it will solve all your problems, but it might provide the idea or the inspiration you need to find the solution.

Above all, this book tries to be *pragmatic*. If it tells you to do something, there's probably a good reason and no sensible short-cut. If there is a known short-cut it'll tell you that, too. It also tries to answer some of the "Why?" questions you may have been afraid to ask!

Should I Be Reading this Book?

A common career progression in computing is to start as a programmer, then become one of several team leaders or junior project managers reporting to a more senior manager, and after that to manage progressively larger projects.

This book is targeted at the team leader or junior project manager getting to grips with the problems of management for the first time. It assumes that the team under your control is quite small (no more than five or six), and there is some more senior guidance and supervision. You may have had a certain amount of management training, but this is by no means always the case, so I don't make too many assumptions.

If you're a more senior manager, or an architect, you should also find something useful in this book (particularly if your own introduction to management was unsupported or informal). The book should clarify your role, may provide some useful ideas and references, and may help if you're involved with a different part of the development life-cycle for the first time.

However, don't expect a wealth of detail on managing large projects. The principles are always the same, but there are methods and tools you can use to manage the volume of information in a large project which are inappropriate for a book of this scope. The "further reading" list may be helpful.

I have tried not to make too many assumptions about the type of systems you're working on, or the languages and methods you use. However, I have to take something as a basis, and I have chosen what I'm most familiar with, which is commercial database systems. These probably represent the bulk of current custom software development, and introduce most of the important management principles. I've also introduced some of the principles of client-server systems and the differences between building and buying systems, also from my own experience. Again, if you develop embedded or real-time systems, for example, some of your analysis and design methods will be quite different, but the management principles are the same.

This little book can't be a substitute for training, experience, or for the advice and assistance which you should get from more senior colleagues, drawing on their experience. Don't be afraid to ask for help or advice, and take the opportunity of training if it presents itself. Also, you'll probably need to consult other books for the detail of particular methods, techniques and standards. However, I hope my book will provide a sound foundation you can build on as your experience grows.

So What's This All About?

A very large number of software projects fail in some way (they are abandoned, end up massively late or over budget, or they just don't get used). A small number of these failures are because the target problems just can't be solved by a computer system, or the technology doesn't work. But the vast majority fail because of problems related to *people* and the way in which they are managed.

If you're going to manage a project, you need to understand these problems, and how to try and prevent them, or to tackle them if they do occur. You need to know how to:

☞   manage your team,

☞   work with your users or customers, and your own managers,

☞   structure, plan and estimate the development work,

☞   make sure the product is properly specified and designed,

☞   manage the build effort, or handle an external supplier,

☞   test and then implement the system for live use.

You will have to communicate with a number of people. Your work could be constrained by standards, methods and procedures. You will have to produce a number of deliverables aside from the code itself. This book is your guide to them.

Questions and Answers

Each chapter tackles a certain aspect of the project manager's job. You'll probably want to read some of them all the way through. However, you may need advice on a particular problem. To help you find it, many of the section headings ask a common question, and the section then tries to answer that question. At the end of each chapter you'll find a summary of the main points, and what you must do.

"Further Reading"

📖   This is an *introductory* book, and can't go into too much detail. However, I've found a number of excellent books which do have more detailed information. A note like this at the end of each chapter, and some sections, will direct you to them, via the "Further Reading" list on page 207.

What Do You Assume I Know?

Not much! You should have a passing familiarity with the basic principles and terminology of software and software development. If you have come to software project management via the usual route of programming (or another development activity) then this will be no problem. If not, see below.

I explain most management terms the first time I use them, but I do assume that you are familiar with very basic terms such as "budget" or "man-day".

What Skills Do I Need?

You *don't* need to be an expert in the technical aspects of the job, but you need to know enough to understand what your team and others are doing, and to work out what management actions to take as a result. If your team can blind you with science, then you either need to learn more, ask different questions, or restructure your team.

Your main tools are the word-processor and the spreadsheet (or pencil and paper). Project management is mostly about people and common sense, not about specialist tools. Communication aids, such as electronic mail, are other key resources. If you have them, then learn how to use them.

To make a good project manager (in any discipline) you need to have a good command of English (or whatever is the dominant language of your organisation). The key role of a manager is to *communicate* - so you must be able to put your ideas into spoken and written words, and understand what others are trying to tell you.

You must also have a good grasp of basic mathematics. There isn't much advanced stuff unless you're going to get into some of the statistical estimating methods, but you do need to be happy with arithmetic. A grasp of concepts like *accuracy* (the range of possible values for an estimate or measurement) will also be of significant benefit.

If you are uncomfortable in these areas, then you may need assistance from someone else - as I explain later, this is not necessarily a bad thing.

📖 If you've come to software project management as an experienced manager but with little software knowledge, then you may need to read an introductory text first: *Software Shock* is a good example. This book, and several of those in the "further reading" section, explain why software development is different from other management tasks: *Peopleware* is also very strong on this topic.

Will You Tell Me About Short-Cuts?

Yes, if I know any. This book concentrates on the principles of project management, and what you *must* do in order to discharge your responsibilities and deliver a properly controlled project. In most cases, you should follow the process through and produce the deliverables described, or some variant of them.

Despite three decades of searching for them, there are no "magic wands" or "silver bullets" which magically reduce the amount of work or skill required to do a good systems development. Such things probably don't actually exist - any one solution or fix concentrates on only part of the life cycle, so the maximum gain (over the whole life cycle) must be fairly small in percentage terms.

However, there are a few tricks you can use to get a useful result quickly, for example in some of the planning activities, and I will describe these guidelines and methods wherever they apply. In some cases the deliverables themselves are optional - you will have to make the decision whether or not such a short-cut is valid in your case.

You shouldn't take other short-cuts unless you are sure you understand their implication, and can reverse any ill effects if necessary. In particular, you must avoid cutting out large amounts of the project documentation - this is always a recipe for later problems, whose cost (in time and money) is much greater than the relatively small initial saving. In the same way, it is usually a mistake to proceed to coding before you are sure about your analysis and design. It may be much more costly to try to convert a prototype into a workable and maintainable system (of the required quality) than to rewrite it from scratch.

The overall message is *"don't take a short-term view"*. Make sure you understand the effects of any decision on your work, and other people's, all the way through the project.

> If in doubt, leave it in!

Instead of a magic wand, there are now a large number of proven methods and tools which provide some improvement in the quality, speed and efficiency of software development. I describe those which I have personally found to be useful, but there are others. This book provides advice on choosing suitable methods and an overall framework for your project. Whatever you choose will still require hard, skilled work, and the application of good management techniques, but the tools and methods should make it easier.

How Does this Book Relate to Structured Methods?

A structured method can bring considerable advantages to the development process:

- A method can define a shape and structure for the development process, so that the various activities are performed in a sensible sequence. It's much easier to do a job if you know what to do and when.

- It may bring a set of techniques and tools which will help you to define the system, and may give you guidance on which techniques to apply and when.

- It may provide templates or contents lists for the various deliverables you must produce.

Note that a structured method is sometimes, wrongly, called a *methodology*. That's a "study of methods", which is what you're doing reading this book. Some people also use the term *formal method*, but it's better to keep that for the mathematical methods used in testing and real-time system design.

There are many different structured methods, some of which are quite general-purpose, and some specific to a particular type of problem or development environment. These may have different structures and terminology, and produce quite different-looking lists of deliverables. However, all are trying to define a sequence of activities which if followed should help you to structure your development logically, get a clear specification, and design and build a good solution to the problem. The deliverables may be structured differently, but the information they'll present is usually the same.

This book isn't tied to any particular method, and it certainly isn't useless if you follow a different one to me. I had to adopt something as a basis, so this book loosely follows a traditional "waterfall" method, using a simple structure with very clear names for things. If you use a different method then you'll have to translate my names for things into the names your method uses, and you may have to do some jobs in a different sequence, or put the results into different documents. I've tried to make this as easy as possible by explaining *why* you need to do a certain job, and what the real product is, quite independent of any particular method.

If you don't use any structured method at present, then this book gives you the outline of a good method to follow. You can get more detail from another book, once you understand the principles clearly.

"He's got an 'Ology"

There are some dangers to structured methods, and if you're going to get the most out of them you need to understand their limitations. Just because someone follows an impressive-sounding "ology" doesn't mean that they are automatically going to get good results - successful development is always the result of intelligent work, properly controlled by a good manager.

The most important thing to realise is that any method is a means to an end, not an end in itself. You need to make sure you understand your eventual target, and how each part of the development process moves you nearer to it. The next chapter discusses how you measure success.

I've often said that *"A structured method, like fire, is a good servant and a very bad master"*. If you find yourself doing things just for the sake of the method or the standards, then ask the question *"why?"*. However, it's probably not a good idea just to ignore the method and standards - there may be a very good reason which will become apparent later. This book should answer the question "why?" for the main steps in any method.

Some methods do demand a lot of paperwork. You will have to strike a balance between too much and too little - there is no one right solution; *you* make the decision, but the answer is not "none" or "tons". The key principle is to understand who will read each document and what they will use it for. Then deliver the information they need, and not too much extra.

Structured methods can also be over-prescriptive. For example, you don't need to use a "prototyping" method to do a bit of prototyping and make good use of the results, but some methods don't allow for this. Many methods only ever talk in terms of completely finishing each stage before moving on, but it can be better to break work up into phases each of which moves through the method in its own right.

Don't be afraid to use some initiative and common sense in applying your method, but remember that there are no magical short-cuts. The method is a tool to make development easier, but you must understand the development process, and make intelligent decisions based on that understanding.

What's Changed in the Second Edition?

This book is mainly about people and what they should do, and most of that hasn't changed much at all! However, since I wrote the first edition of this book eight years ago a lot has changed in IT, and this edition reflects those changes.

The methods have changed. Iterative and incremental development methods are now more common than the old-fashioned "waterfall" approaches. There are many less formal "Rapid Application Development" approaches, such as *DSDM* and *eXtreme Programming*, which aim to develop systems with less modelling and documentation. I compare these, and provide some guidance on where you might use them.

Object-oriented development was *an* option eight years ago, but most people were doing something else. Now it's the most common approach for new systems, and the focus of my examples. In the same way the Unified Modelling Language (UML) has become the standard for system modelling, and I've updated my models to use it.

The importance of software architecture and the role of the architect are now much better understood. I've extended the Design section to include a number of modern architecture ideas, and design "best practices" which increase your chance of success:

♦ Design patterns, a way of re-using proven design and programming solutions,

♦ Component-based and service-based architectures, which help you to divide a development up, and make better use of existing systems,

♦ Multi-tier architectures, the modern way of structuring systems so that different developers concentrate on different concerns,

♦ Application integration ideas, technologies and standards,

♦ Allowing users to directly manipulate problems via expressive user interfaces.

We understand much better now than eight years ago that systems don't stand alone, they have to be *integrated* with others, and that we have to plan for growth and change. I discuss these issues, and the strategies you should follow to address them.

Finally, I've changed. In the last eight years I've taken on lots of different roles as an independent consultant. I've seen various successes and problems, and if as a result I can improve the advice I gave eight years ago, I've tried to do so.

Acknowledgements

A book like this is never just the work of one person, and I want to thank all those who have helped me to create it.

The progenitor of this book was an internal document created during my time as Information Services Quality Manager at Eurotunnel. I must particularly thank my co-author on that document, **Sue German**, for all her help, advice and inspiration, and her permission to use it as the seed for this book. I must also thank **Dave Pointon** and **Paul Bassat** of Eurotunnel for their encouragement and support during my time there, and for their permission to re-use some of my work.

Two other major contributions came from **Mary Hazeltine**, who proof-read and improved the English of both editions, and my wife **Frances**, who has been unceasing in her support and encouragement.

The anecdotes, warnings and examples in this book come from a number of sources, but my close friend **Stephen Hazeltine** and my father **Martin Johnston** probably contributed more than their fair share. Both are sadly no longer with us, and their support, humour and inspiration are sadly missed.

Paul Herzlich and **Cindy Morelli** of Système Evolutif Ltd. contributed to the work at Eurotunnel, and also started me on the book writing trail. They must take their share of the blame! My friends and ex-colleagues **Nigel Woodhead** and **Roger Nickless** contributed both ideas and practical assistance to the creation of this book. For their encouragement and practical help in reviewing my work, thanks.

A number of people reviewed this book during its draft stages: **Sue**, **Nigel**, **Steve**, **Cindy**, **David Fletcher** and **Bill Hetzel** for the first edition, **Marc Sewell** and **John Levett** for the second edition. Thanks to all of you.

Thanks are also due to my publisher **Mike Cash** at Butterworth-Heinemann, to **Sarah Ward** of the same company for her excellent cartoons, and to my sister-in-law **Helen Floate** for extending Sarah's work for the second edition.

This book builds, quite unashamedly, on the work of others in the field, for all of whom I have the greatest admiration. To **Fred Brooks**, **Tom DeMarco**, **Tim Lister**, **Edward Yourdon** and many others - thanks for your ideas!

And finally, thanks and humble apologies to anyone who I have inadvertently missed off the list.

Success and Failure

A great number of software projects fail. They fail in many different ways, for example:

- ● the developers fail to deliver,

- ● the software is delivered, but late and full of errors,

- ● the users refuse to use the software,

- ● the users use the software, but it fails to improve their business, or to meet their business needs.

These standards of success and failure aren't absolute - one party may judge a project a success, but another will judge it a failure.

There are even more reasons for failure than types of failure. Technical problems may cause a project to fail, but it's more likely that the problem is with the management of the project (by you, your users or your managers). Typical problems include:

- ☹ failure to agree or understand the requirements,

- ☹ failure to correctly estimate and plan the project, both as a whole and in stages,

- ☹ failure to control progress and keep effort directed at the right goals,

- ☹ failure to recognise and manage risks early enough.

As the project manager, you need to be clear minded, and understand how the success of your project will be judged. You then need to manage risks and control the project to maximise your chance of achieving your goals. This chapter discusses why projects fail, and then goes on to define the basic principles for ensuring success.

Why Do Software Projects Fail?

Depending on which books you read, somewhere between a quarter and three quarters of all software projects fail in some sense or other: the software is never delivered, it's delivered but is late and full of errors, the users refuse to use the software, or they use it but can't get any business benefit from it. Some studies have suggested that as few as two percent of software projects deliver on time, to budget, and at a quality level sufficient to make good use of the software quickly.

There are all sorts of reasons why projects fail. A full list is impossible, but most of the problems fall into a few main categories:

1. *Over-ambition*. The users try to make the system do too much. This can cause failure because the user organisation isn't ready for the new way of working, or can't accommodate the changes quickly enough. The users may expect a level of functionality and quality incompatible with the budget. In the worst case, the requirements may simply exceed some intrinsic limitation of the environment or technology (or even a physical law). Alternatively, sometimes the real load on the system is underestimated, and the system just isn't able to support it.

2. *Over-complexity*. This is similar to over-ambition, but is more often the fault of the developers, who will try to include too many features or use more complex technology than required. The failure occurs either when the users cannot use the system, or when the software can't be practically maintained.

3. *Bad planning*. In a very real sense, *all* failures are evidence of inadequate planning and control. However, a significant proportion can be traced back directly to such causes as an unrealistic plan, failure to notice slippage, or panic when it is realised the plan won't be met.

4. *People factors*. Lots of failures occur because people can't (or just *won't*) work effectively together. A poor working environment or bad leadership may be the cause, or there may be political problems leading to conflicting objectives and requirements.

5. *Bad communication and mis-understandings*. Another common problem is a failure to communicate. The users may fail to communicate what they want, the analysts may fail to understand, or the developers may fail to communicate what they are intending to do. If the project manager fails to communicate properly with his team, the users or his managers, then a major problem is almost guaranteed.

6. *"Wicked problems"*. Some problems don't lend themselves to solution by a classic software development. For example, it may not be clear what the right solution is, there's no easy way to test each solution and the cost of a wrong solution may be enormous or permanent. Some software projects fail because the users and developers don't understand these constraints.

7. *Inadequate skills*. In some cases, the project team don't have the necessary technical or management skills. This can be rectified by training, but not in an arbitrarily short time or at zero cost.

8. *Uncontrolled changes*. It's impossible to hit a moving goal. Changes to the requirements and plans must be properly managed for any hope of success.

9. *External supply*. An external supplier may fail to deliver for any or all of the above reasons, but is essentially outside the direct control of the project manager. Good formal project management techniques are vital in this case.

10. *Failure to recognise risks*. Sometimes, when development seems to be going well, one unfortunate incident causes it to collapse. For example, a key developer is taken ill, and no-one can take over from him. It is irresponsible to assume that no such events will occur, and if the risks aren't managed any one may be enough to cause the project to fail.

Most of these aren't technical problems, and even those which are due to a "technical" cause might be avoided or controlled by better management. Any one of these problems may be enough to cause the development to fail. In other cases, the development will suffer in many ways because of "knock-on" effects from a few basic shortcomings.

It may seem impossible to avoid these problems, and a miracle that any useful software ever gets created. However, some sensible precautions can avoid a lot of trouble. That's the aim of the rest of this book, based on the following strategy:

☺   Make sure the requirements are clearly understood.

☺   Plan well.

☺   Identify and manage risks.

☺   Track progress against the plan(s).

☺   Communicate with everyone.

So How Do I Know If I've Succeeded?

You are trying to make your development *succeed*, but what is success? It's very easy to say that you have succeeded if you have avoided an obvious failure, but this may not be enough.

There is a contract between the developers and the users which has five main aspects:

Functional requirements   what the system must *do* (to meet the business's needs),

Technical requirements   how the system must work,

Quality requirements   how well the system must work, and possibly the process by which the system must be built,

Plan   the schedule of milestones and deliveries,

Budget   the cost of the work, in effort and/or money terms.

If you have achieved all these, you may well (and quite deservedly), view your work as a success. Conversely, failure to meet any of these targets *may* mean complete failure. Of course, what's more likely to happen is that you will achieve some of the targets (or very nearly), but won't be so close to the others.

There is a further complication. If you have built the wrong system (that is, to the "wrong" requirements) then it may be a good system but still be of no benefit to the business, and the users won't agree with your definition of success.

To avoid this problem, you must ensure that all the parties to the development agree, at a very early stage, a set of key indicators for the project's success. These must be measurable, objective indicators, not subjective opinions. For example, "The system must be easy to use" is meaningless, whereas "A secretary who knows the old system should be able to work unsupported after one hour's training" is a firm, testable requirement, and could be used as a criterion for success.

You therefore need to understand the way in which the successful system will change or improve the business, or how the overall success of the business operations involving software will be judged. If it's going to replace an existing way of working, it may be worth measuring the cost or efficiency of the situation before the system is introduced, so that you can make a real comparison afterwards. If possible, it's much easier to agree on things which the users can measure themselves, or which come out of normal measures of the business's performance.

What's the Importance of Measuring Things?

You need to be able to *prove*, by an objective "yes" or "no" answer, whether or not you have met the requirements for the project. Some of the requirements are yes/no by their very nature (either the system can perform function X, or it can't), but many are not so clear.

However, if you can measure something, you can set a target for it, and give a "yes" or "no" answer whether you've met your target. Otherwise, you can't give that answer. It's as simple as that!

> "You can't control what you can't measure."
> Tom DeMarco
> (after Lord Kelvin)

Furthermore, if you are trying to control the progress of the project, you must be able to evaluate properly how much is done, and how much left to do. A proper measurement will help you to do this, whereas "finger in the air" guesses of "90% complete" are meaningless.

You *can* measure anything if you put your mind to it. The measurement may not be free or even cheap, and it may not be perfect, but it will always be better than nothing. In the rest of this book, I try to suggest simple measurements you can make to give you much greater control over the project.

What are "Critical Success Factors"?

During the acceptance process, you'll have to check whether you have satisfied a large number of requirements. It's very useful (essential if you want a clear indication of success and failure) to identify a few key targets which you *must* meet. These are the "critical success factors" for the project.

Ideally, you should express these in terms of the user's business, or in terms of very visible attributes of your project such as total cost or final delivery date. However, they might well include quality attributes, such as the mean time between failures, or the average time to fix a bug. They probably won't include many pure functional requirements, since you *should* be able to meet any particular functional requirement. (I'll discuss how to grade the importance of requirements in the "Analysis" chapter.)

When you've delivered the software, and performed any start-up or implementation work, you then need to measure how successfully the software is being used, against the critical success factors. If you have achieved all of them, then you have succeeded. If not, you know where to concentrate your efforts. In some cases, you can even start measuring things against these targets before delivery, which will give you yet greater control of your project.

Prevention and Cure

Prevention is almost always better than cure, and this is nowhere more true than in project management. An important feature of any well-run and successful project is regular checks for potential problems, and attempts to avoid or work around them as soon as they are detected.

If you don't undertake such checks, you won't spot the problems until they are well advanced, which may be too late! It is almost impossible to recover lost time or to patch up a system based on an inadequate plan, specification or design, so it's much better to try to avoid these problems if you can.

The following key points make up a strategy for problem prevention:

🔔 *Regular reviews*. These have to start early enough to make a difference, and with the aim of finding problems and fixing them. There's absolutely no point whatsoever holding reviews after the work is completed, or if you have already moved on to the next stage of work with no intention of changing what you are doing if a problem is found. Include independent reviewers, with both technical and user viewpoints if you can.

🔔 *Communication*. Talk to people. Make it clear that there is praise, not punishment, if someone identifies a potential problem and tells you about it. *Don't shoot the messenger!*

🔔 *Progress checks*. As project manager, you need to be continually comparing progress with the plan. This is much easier to do if you have lots of real, identifiable milestones and measure progress towards them.

🔔 ***Early*** *testing and inspection*. Testing will help build confidence in your system, and help to prove that you are in control.

🔔 *Risk Analysis*. It is a good idea to list potential problems, and evaluate what

> "A stitch in time saves nine" obviously a "soft-wear" engineer

their impact would be, and how likely they are to occur. You can then develop solutions to the greatest risks, and a contingency plan. Details of this process are in the "How Do I Spot Problems?" section on page 38.

What Do I Have to Deliver?

There should be a number of defined, tangible products from the development work. These are known as *deliverables*. Obviously the working system makes one or more of these, but there should be a number of others, which will probably be documents.

As well as being the actual solid products of your work, the deliverables fulfil two very useful roles: they are valuable as communication tools, and they provide firm checks on the project's progress. You can tie estimates, plans and payments to the delivery of the first version of each deliverable, and (even better) to the delivery of the tested or reviewed version which the user or customer accepts.

If you orient your work towards deliverables in this way, you will have much clearer indications of success or failure. You will also avoid the subjective evaluation which is always a problem if you concentrate, instead, on the services you provide.

You can always define your work in terms of deliverables. For example, if you are doing maintenance work, look at how you can batch up fixes into regular deliveries. If you are testing, you can deliver a test report with a list of the errors found.

You must always understand who is the user of each deliverable. Know your audience, and deliver what will be most useful to them (and not much more!). Don't create deliverables for their own sake or to keep the QA Manager happy, but think about the purpose of each deliverable, and concentrate on creating something which meets that purpose. If you find this difficult to do because the deliverable seems to have more than one purpose, then consider splitting it into two or more parts.

Keep your eyes on the prize! Don't get side-tracked into producing massive intermediate documents which no-one will read. Again, think about the purpose of the deliverable, and concentrate on the most efficient way of meeting that purpose.

Most, but not all, deliverables will need to be updated when other parts of the system change. Understanding the audience and purpose of the deliverable will help you decide what needs to be updated. The easier the update, the more likely it is to happen. Aim for a clear, simple, structured and focussed deliverable which can be updated relatively easily.

So How Do I Ensure Success?

1. A large number of software projects fail. They fail in many ways, and for a large number of reasons, but most of these are to do with the management of people, rather than technical problems.

2. Understand how the success of your project will be judged. Agree, at a very early stage, the key indicators of success for the project as a whole. Think about how you can *measure* the success of the system from a business perspective.

3. Make sure the requirements are clearly understood and agreed. Remember that these include the technical and quality requirements, and the constraints of budget and time, as well as the functional requirements.

4. Plan well, and early. Track your progress against the plan and report in the same terms. Do not change your plan without consultation.

5. Prevention is better than cure. Understand the reasons why projects fail. Take time to identify the possible risks, and create contingency plans for any which are either very likely or which could endanger the project's success. Good progress checking and reporting is the only way of trapping problems before they become too serious.

6. Define the deliverables from your work, and concentrate on them. Make sure you know the purpose and audience of each deliverable, and that you match the deliverable to its purpose.

7. Communicate with everyone. The most common cause of failure for software projects is because someone (or many people) don't understand what is happening, and what they (and others) are supposed to be doing. Clear, regular communication is the only way to solve this, and it's *your* responsibility.

📖 *Peopleware, Software Project Management,* and *Wicked Problems, Righteous Solutions* all have a good discussion of why projects fail. *AntiPatterns* contains a number of early indicators of trouble. *Software Project Management* has a very good section on risk management, as does *Principles of Software Engineering Management.* That book, *Why Does Software Cost So Much?* and *Controlling Software Projects* are all very strong on the use of *metrics* (ways of measuring things).

The Art of Project Management

You won't be able to do all the tasks in a development yourself. Usually, you will have a team working with you, perhaps an external supplier, and you will also have to get what you need from the users and your managers. To fulfil your task you will have to manage, either directly or indirectly, the efforts of all these people. Essentially you must:

> *Lead!*

> *Plan!*

> *Communicate!*

> *Build the team!*

> *Get things done!*

This chapter is about how to manage people to achieve your project's objectives.

I assume that, as a newcomer to project management, you're going to be leading a relatively small project, or a team within a larger project. The principles are the same for larger projects, but there are some detailed techniques you'll need to learn, and you'll need to gain practical experience with a smaller job first.

What Does a Project Manager Do?

I've met many people who seem to think that project management is about solving problems of someone else's creation, like Tommy Lee Jones's character. However, I'd say that if this is your situation, then you're either a top trouble-shooter, or you haven't managed the projects properly.

> "I got tired of coming up with last minute, desperate solutions to impossible problems created by other ●˙♨⚘✳ing people!"
> Tommy Lee Jones in "Under Siege"

To avoid ending up like this, there are a number of things you have to do, regularly and effectively, starting with your first involvement in the project:

> *Leading and building the team.* Co-ordinate the activities of a group of people, so that things happen in the right way and at the right time. Perhaps even more importantly, you need to co-ordinate their different *goals*. If they have a common objective, they will deploy their own efforts more effectively. Your aim is to build a team whose ability as a whole is much greater than the sum of its parts.

> *Planning.* Every task on the project, and the use of every resource (including people), should be planned in advance. Otherwise, you will either under-use your valuable resources, or you will have insufficient resources and the project will slip. As well as managing time and effort, you have to manage the quality of the work which is done, and allow for things which could go wrong. You will have to regularly update your estimates and plans as circumstances change.

> *Communicating.* Everyone must understand what is being done, by whom and why, and this is down to communication skills. You need to open up as many communication channels as possible, and make regular use of them.

> *Monitoring and reporting progress.* Constantly monitor progress (against your plan), spot problems quickly, and report on your progress to your users and managers. If you do this, and particularly if you can suggest practical solutions to the problems, then others will have greater confidence in you, and you will get approval for your work more easily.

> *Getting things done!* Understand your overall objectives (and the intermediate deliverables), and progress towards them.

What are the Key Skills of a Project Manager?

Planning and *communicating* are the two key skills essential for success in project management. Like any other skill they can be learned, and will improve with practice. Don't be afraid to admit that you may need help with them. Watch those who do them well, and ask for advice. You can also learn a lot from books or training courses, but these are no substitute for experience!

Make sure that every part of the project is represented in a documented plan. Remember, a plan is only complete if you can answer the six key questions *what?*, *why?*, *when?*, *where?*, *how?* and *who?*.

I keep six honest serving men,
They taught me all I knew,
Their names are What, and Why, and When,
And Where, and How, and Who.

Rudyard Kipling

If *you* can answer these questions, check that your team, your manager and your users can answer them too. Make your plan one of your ways of communicating with people – it's not just something produced to satisfy moaning management with nothing better to do than to chase you for useless deliverables!

Keep asking people what they are doing, what progress they are making (against the relevant plan), and tell them what you (and the rest of the team) are doing. There are various ways this can be done: formal, written reports are essential, but verbal reports and memos are also useful. Don't, for example, wait until monthly report time to tell your managers about a developing problem which may need their help to sort out!

Note that I haven't said anything about analysing, designing or programming. These are not project management jobs. *You* need to make sure that they happen, and are done properly, but it is not essential for you to do everything. Indeed, you must avoid the situation where the real project management jobs are left undone because you're concentrating too much on the technical problems. Remember, you don't have to be a technical expert to manage a project. It's sometimes said that "management is the art of delegation" - more about this later.

In a small team, you will have some technical tasks (and you may be more experienced technically than the people you're managing). That's fine, but then you must plan your time carefully: some will be dedicated to your technical tasks, but some (quite separate, and planned) *must* be *dedicated* to managing the project.

How Do I Lead?

First, make sure that the overall objectives of the project are clear, and communicate these to the team: *focus on a common goal.* Develop and communicate plans which detail the tasks and individual goals of the team (and those around them). Finally, make sure that the work is being done and goals met, and communicate this progress against the plan back to IS management and the users.

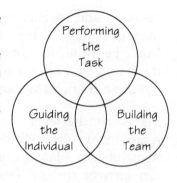

Leadership

Leadership is often portrayed as a three-part process: performing the task, guiding and building the skills of the individuals in the team, and building the team as a whole. The results of the team should be greater than the sum of the results from its parts.

How Do I Get People to Do Things?

You should have a certain amount of authority over people working within your team because of your position, but this doesn't necessarily mean they will follow your instructions. Other people, outside your project team, will also have to contribute to the success of the project, but you have no authority over them at all. Thus you can't rely on orders. Instead, you have to persuade people to fulfil their tasks willingly.

Try to understand what motivates people in general, and each member of your team in particular. The most powerful motivators for most people are recognition, achievement and appreciation - not physical rewards like money (as long as the latter are adequate). This is good news for you: unless you're quite senior you can't do much about the salaries of your team, but you can make clear, formal and public recognition of their efforts and achievements. You'll find that even a mention by name in your progress report will get you some good will, and with a bit of ingenuity you can do much more than that.

Study what can de-motivate people. Don't assume that completing the task or improving the company's business are the prime objectives of all your team members - they aren't. You need to understand what drives each person, and what they want out of life as a whole. For example, you may have two very good workers, one who has a busy (but cheap) social life, and one who has an expensive but solitary hobby. The latter will happily do lots of overtime, but the former will probably be very unwilling if you don't take his other arrangements into account.

Find ways of aligning individual objectives with the team's. Seek out what the objectives of each person are, then clearly communicate the team's objectives and explain how meeting those objectives will result in progress towards the individual ones. For example, successful work on this project might put them first in line for work on a much more interesting project starting in a few months' time - this sort of promise (if honoured) is a very strong motivator.

You won't always be able to align all the objectives, particularly if the project is under real pressure to deliver. If you can't, then the project's objectives should come first. However, following the same principles may make a bitter pill a bit easier to swallow.

Beware of conflicting pressures. A programmer who should do something to improve quality but is late has two opposing negative pressures: criticism for either poor quality or late delivery. He will take the action which is "least negative", probably the poor quality route. If this isn't what you want, then, in the words of the song, you have to "Accentuate the positive, eliminate the negative" and create an environment in which a balance of motivations achieves what you want.

How Do I Allocate Work?

Divide the work up into separate tasks, each with a clear objective. You should then allocate these to people who have some reasonable chance of success. Try to give people a fair mix of the boring and interesting jobs, and allow them to grow by giving them a bit of a challenge (but not one they have no chance of meeting). Try as well to balance the work-load - don't overload your best people leaving the less able with nothing to do. (See the section on Planning and Estimating for more details.)

Don't be afraid to delegate. Sharing your tasks with other members of the team helps them to learn and understand what is going on, and may be essential if your own workload is too large. However, delegation does not mean that you abandon responsibility for the task. You must establish that the plans are being met and the quality is adequate - you have to *plan*, and spend time to monitor the work and possibly educate your team.

Make sure you can assess the quality and completeness of every deliverable. If you can't do it personally, get another member of the team, or even an outsider, to do so. If you have an independent QA group, or there's another project team working on a similar project, ask them to participate in the reviews and inspections.

If you follow these rules, and create the right motivation by matching the individual and team objectives, there's a good chance that your team will accept their tasks by consensus, and you won't need to give *orders* at all.

What if People Make Mistakes?

Recognise that everyone's human, and errors do occur. Don't be too defensive. However, don't create an environment in which sloppy work is acceptable. Instead try to create an atmosphere in which errors can be freely discussed, and where the identification of a problem creates a joint responsibility for the "finder" and "owner" to correct the problem and to prevent its recurrence. This must be even-handed - don't be afraid to submit your work for review by members of your team, or others.

Don't try to correct things that you might be slightly unhappy with, unless they are actually errors. The fact that you can think of a better way of doing something is not necessarily a reason for change. Remember that all changes cost time and money, and may impact the team's ability to meet its objectives. It's also very difficult for a more junior team member to make progress if his work is constantly being replaced by his seniors' "better ideas".

Be aware of the possible impact of poor design decisions or inadequate analysis on the project. Some such errors (which have probably been made by more senior members of the team) could prove fatal if not corrected early enough. The question to ask in these cases is not "can it be done better?" but "what are the risks if we adopt this approach?". In the case of poor analysis or design the risks will be unacceptably high, and you must manage them by working together to find a better way. Similarly, code or documentation which will cause problems for other people needs to be rectified. You must allow for some individuality - people aren't machines - but this must not be at the cost of maintainability or control.

On a practical note, most people will do a job in the easiest way. If you want to work to standards, then a small investment in simple tools and templates (for example to create a standard screen form, or for standard documents) will dramatically improve the chance of their acceptance.

The creation (and promotion) of the right attitude to errors is essential. Some errors will occur, and are probably essential if the team and its members are to learn. However, they should be identified by the review and testing processes, and corrected in a precise and non-personal way. Nothing is more demotivating for the team than to think that any old rubbish is acceptable. Allow the product to rise to a level of quality which satisfies the team - this *will* be productive.

Ultimately, you have to trust your people. Don't try to over-prescribe their actions. It won't work, and you will lose more in lost enthusiasm and motivation than you will ever regain in control.

How Do I Build a Team?

If you're lucky, then the members of your project team will start to work together in a way that will make the team more successful than the individuals working togther. There will be a clear common objective, and work will be directed effectively towards that objective. You may find there is a certain amount of unspoken communication, with a greater common understanding than usual. This is a very enjoyable and productive experience. It is often described as a team *jelling*.

There's no simple, foolproof way to make a team jell, but you can set up the right environment, take sensible steps towards building the team, and hope for the best.

Team building starts with having an open framework in which everyone understands what he is doing and how it fits into the whole, and in which you can publicly discuss progress and problems. Try to build an identity for your team - your planning and reporting should be on behalf of the team, not "your" project. Encourage your team to behave as a unit: going for a drink or a meal together can often help build team spirit, and open up the channels of communication.

There are certain things you need to avoid if you're going to have any chance of making a team work effectively together. Defensive management and a bad attitude to errors and the quality of the product is one: see the previous page. Excessive bureaucracy and paper-heavy development is another: you should try to get the whole team to understand the principles of targeting each deliverable and delivering just what the target audience needs.

It's almost impossible to build teams if the members are physically separated, or if each member's time is fragmented between a number of jobs. It's worth fighting battles with your management for a good working environment in which the whole team can work properly together. A lot of the research suggests that the working environment is the only factor which consistently affects quality and productivity. A good working environment has to include *quiet* space for the high-concentration activities such as programming or writing, and separate space for people to work together without disturbing the rest.

📖 You can't *make* a team jell, but you can provide the right environment. This section (and the next one) are an introduction to the most important principles. Read *Peopleware* if you really want to manage people and teams properly. The working environment is one of the most important factors, and may not be under your control. If your managers won't do something about a poor environment, try to get them to read *Peopleware* too!

How Do I Make Sure the Team is Complete?

In order to achieve its main objectives, your team has to do a lot of separate things. These tasks won't all appear on your official list of tasks in your plan, but they need to happen nonetheless if your team is going to succeed:

❧ *Leadership.* Someone (probably you) needs to align the goals of the team members with the team's own objectives, and provide direction towards those objectives. On a larger project, you'll need other leaders for each separate part.

❧ *Decision making.* Someone needs to make decisions when necessary. This needn't be the same person all the time, and needn't always be a single person. In some of the best teams, there is some form of collective decision making, but the leader has to be able to make and follow a decision if the collective process doesn't work for any reason.

❧ *Team building.* This is one task you can't make explicit ("Alice, you're in charge of making sure the team jells this week!"), but you will often find that someone takes charge of arranging little social events, or smoothing over ruffled feathers! If you have such a person, who may just act as a catalyst for the other members of the team to sort things out, then it's invaluable.

❧ *Communication.* As we've discussed, this is key to a successful development.

❧ *Selling the products of the team.* I don't mean the external sales of what you have produced, but the effort of proving to management and users that what you have produced is what they want and asked for. This is closely allied to communication, and may be done by the same person, as part of the same tasks.

- *Ensuring technical coherence.* Someone needs to own the high-level design (or architecture), check it is being followed and check that the elements fit together into a coherent whole. From the conception of the solution and the basic design through to integration with other systems, someone has to understand the structure and communicate it to other people. This role of software architect is so important I devote a whole section to it later in the book.

- *Planning.* Someone needs to create and maintain the plans and estimates.

- *Productivity and progress checking.* You need to make regular checks on the progress of each activity against the plan(s). If you are trying to *measure* your achievements, someone needs to be in charge of the measurements. Someone needs to make sure that you meet your targets, and jobs are actually finished - the formal announcement of targets met can have a very positive effect.

- *Quality checking.* Each component or deliverable has to be checked against its specification. Someone other than the object's creator should do this checking, and you will find that some people have much better checking skills than others, just as some are better programmers or writers.

- *Documentation.* Even if you're careful with the paperwork load, there's a lot of documentation to be created and maintained.

- *Administrative & secretarial functions.*

These tasks require a range of personality traits and skills that you won't find in any one person, so you need to build a similar variety into your team. Take advantage of the different strengths within people. If you are aware that your own communication skills are not as good as those of another team member, involve him or her in helping you to write and present reports.

Be sensible with the documentation and administrative functions. If you're lucky enough to have a professional administrator, then use him or her. If not, share the admin. tasks, but make sure they get done. Whatever you do, don't tie up your best technical resources in paperwork, just because they've risen to the "senior" position of team leader.

Leadership and management skills can be learned, but don't exist just because of seniority or experience. Don't promote a good engineer to be a poor team leader.

Together with your managers, you are responsible for staffing your team. Look at the list of tasks above, and make sure that someone in the team is tackling each one. If not, you have a profile for the missing members of your team.

How Do I Plan, Report and Communicate?

How do I know if I'm communicating properly?

Talk to people. Spend some time just talking through the job with each member of your team, your managers and your users.

Concentrate on making communication effective: see if your team, your managers and your users can answer questions *you* ask them about *your* plans. If they can, then you are succeeding. If not, then you may need to try something different.

Be aware that typically you only remember 20% of what you hear, 30% of what you read, but about 50% of what you both hear and read. Thus you should try to have both written and oral communication together: *always* write a confirmation of a discussion, telephone call or meeting, and whenever practical follow up a written communication with a verbal clarification. This is particularly important if your team has a mixture of first languages, or widely differing communication skills. It's also useful in resolving disputes, and essential when working with external suppliers.

In written material, make sure that the structure is clear so that people can refer to it more than once - they may need to try to find the 50% they haven't remembered! When you're dealing with your users this is very important - the style of communication may be different but the rules should be exactly the same.

Make the most of meetings. Make sure every meeting has a clear agenda and objectives. Use them to build joint understanding of the problems and objectives, and to reach a consensus about the way forward. *Do* allow constructive discussion of relevant topics, but *don't* allow your precious time to be chewed up by arguments or technical discussions between two or three people - the simple solution is just to suggest that this is a topic for another meeting. At the end of the meeting, sum up what you believe has been agreed. Make sure that every meeting has minutes - if one of your team does the minutes you can also check (when you review them) that he has understood the main messages of the meeting. An *absolute minimum* is to document the action points and anything you have agreed on!

There's no set list of meetings you must have (although one may be dictated by your management or a contract). However, you should aim to have at least a weekly progress meeting with your team, which should have *documented* actions and policy decisions. You should also meet formally with your managers and (maybe separately) the users every month, and compare progress with your plan. Again, you should produce minutes stating what you have agreed, and who has what action points.

How Do I Plan?

Creating a plan is a separate topic (to which another chapter is dedicated). The trick is that you must try and identify every task required to complete the project. Then, for every task, you must be able to answer the six key questions *What?*, *Why?*, *When?*, *Where? How?* and *Who?*. If you can't answer all these questions by reading the plan, then it isn't complete.

In an effective plan the individual tasks must be broken up enough that they are fairly short (i.e. a few days), and there must be a clear yes/no or numeric measure of success. Then you can either be sure that a task is actually complete, or you can trap slippage early on.

How Do I Know What Progress I'm Making?

Once you have a plan, you need to report your progress against it. The most important thing here is to be absolutely truthful: be proud of your successes, but honest about your failures and any problems you may be having. If others know, they may be able to help, but if you hide the true state of affairs then by the time the problems come to light it may be too late to do anything about them! Know when to get help - there is nothing unusual, and no shame, in having problems and needing assistance, but you will fail as a project manager if you don't accept this.

Talk to your team and find out how they are progressing, *against the plan*. *Use* the plan as an active tool, not as a dead report which you have to update for your managers' benefit. Get regular status reports from every member of the team (listing their progress, plan and problems). These should only take them about 20 minutes to write, or they don't understand their plan. You can then use these in your own report.

Be sceptical. For work in progress, ask "How long to complete", not "How much have you done". Don't fall into the trap of the old saying... For a job which is supposed to be finished, check that *all* the finishing off has been done (including any paperwork or

> The first 90% of the development takes 90% of the time. The remaining 10% takes the other 90% of the time

delivery procedures) and you can *prove* the targets for that component have been reached. If you have an independent testing or QA team, then look for verification of progress from them.

Make sure that the users, your manager and your team are aware of any changes to the objectives or the deadlines. There is nothing worse than to waste time because someone has not understood that the priorities have changed.

How Do I Gain Management Approval and Confidence?

Earlier in the chapter, I discussed how to create an environment in which you can trust your team to work effectively, with some tolerance of problems providing they are properly handled. Create a similar relationship with your managers, as otherwise your own efforts will be hampered. The following suggestions will help you to create a reasonable relationship, although they cannot be guaranteed since so much is down to personal preferences and styles.

A stream of deliverables on time and to the requirements will produce confidence in you. This is one good reason for creating a number of interim deliverables, and delivering the system in phases, with simple, low-risk items being delivered early. A method for structuring the project this way is in the chapter "Structuring the Development".

Unfortunately, you won't always be able to achieve this. The project structure may not suit this approach, or you may run into problems. The key to creating management confidence is good reporting and a clear information flow. There are no prizes for hiding problems, but if you spot and report them early, together with a possible solution, then your managers should be happy that you are in control.

How Do I Introduce Proper Methods?

You may have a more difficult problem: you want to use proper methods and run the project as this book tells you to, but your managers may not support this. The following arguments are often offered against use of proper methods:

- *The method is too theoretical, and won't work in the "real world"*. The answer to this is that unstructured "real world" techniques fail too often.

- *Everything has to be written down - there's too much documentation*. There can be a grain of truth in this, as I've said earlier. However, good written communication is *essential*. A sensible level of paperwork will often save a lot of wasted time. The trick is to find a balance, by properly targeting deliverables and written communications.

- *We have always managed without lengthy procedures before*. If this is true, and all the earlier developments have been successful, fine. In truth, there is probably plenty of evidence that the informal developments have had their fair share of problems. If you can, investigate the true situation, but avoid creating ill feeling if your researches show too many past failures!

- *These are good methods, but we can't afford to implement them now*. Why not? If the informal methods are causing failed projects, and therefore wasting time and money, you may not be able to afford *not* to implement them. If it's a question of developer training and learning curves, then you need to concentrate on a few relatively small, high-benefit changes.

A lot depends on the maturity of your software organisation. Surveys have shown that about 90% of software organisations are in a state best described as *initial* or *chaotic*. There is little formalisation of the development process, with only ad-hoc controls and irregular use of tools and standards. Some developments do succeed, but success is neither repeatable nor measured. Other organisations do have a more formal development process and some technical standards, but very few (if any) have reached the optimised, measured quality regime of the best in other industries.

The only way to move up from the chaotic level is to introduce good basic project and quality management practices. Advanced technology (such as better CASE tools, or complicated methods) won't help much, and even if it does solve some problems the improvement won't be measurable, repeatable or general across the organisation. In the worst case, attempting to make big changes to an immature organisation by using a particular new tool or technique could cause drastic problems. If you're in that position then all you can do is concentrate on good basic project management.

On the other hand, if you're lucky enough to work in an organisation with defined management standards, then work within the existing framework. Concentrate on changes to things like methods and technical standards, fitting them into the existing practices.

You have to make your changes fit the corporate culture. Changes are easier to adopt if they can be understood in the context of what already exists. For example, if your organisation makes good use of electronic mail, don't try to introduce a method based on paper forms. The corporate culture will also affect activities like team building and your leadership style. If possible, try to work within the spirit of the organisation and make a series of small changes, rather than large changes which are likely to be unacceptable. If there are a lot of other changes happening in the organisation, then it's probably not a good time to make too many changes of your own.

Explain to the managers *why* some things must change. Try to fit the changes to the current corporate culture. They should then support you. If, however, there is no prospect of long-term improvements then you may be better off elsewhere.

📖 *The Decline and Fall of the American Programmer* discusses at length the SEI software process maturity model, and what you have to do to move up it.

How Expert Do I Have to Be?

You don't have to be an expert in technical matters to be a good software project manager. As we've already seen, most of the problems are related to the management of people, and you won't solve these by technical solutions. Instead, you have to concentrate on managing the people: by understanding their needs and objectives, by creating and maintaining the right management framework, and by leading, planning and communicating.

You don't even have to be an expert in management techniques. Most of the approaches in this book require some common sense and sensitivity, but the detailed methods are quite straightforward and don't need any great tool support or prior knowledge. Obviously your ability will grow with experience, you need to constantly evaluate and improve your skills in communication, estimating, planning and man-management, and you may need to get help from time to time, but you can start from quite a low baseline.

However, this doesn't mean that you can succeed without any technical knowledge at all. There are a number of things you must be able to do which need a combination of technical and management skills:

◎ *You have to be able to evaluate the accuracy of information given to you.* You may have a team member who says "I can't do it because...", or you may have to arbitrate between two conflicting technical views. In these and many other cases, you'll either need to understand the technicalities, or find a way of reducing the information to a form you can understand.

◎ *You must understand what's going on.* You have to report on behalf of the team to users and managers. You must therefore be able to understand the state of the project. In some cases, you will also have to translate quite technical reports so that less technical people will understand them.

◎ *You may have to provide guidance.* It's unlikely that a developer will expect you to provide a detailed solution (if you don't have the technical expertise), but you will sometimes be asked for guidance.

◎ *You must be sure that instructions are practical and estimates realistic.*

◎ *You must understand how good progress is.* If you want to avoid the "90% complete" syndrome, you must understand what has actually been achieved, and, more importantly, what you still have to do.

The following strategy may help you deal with those problems where you don't understand the technical detail:

1. Make sure you understand the software production process. A lot of questions will be answered by the team themselves if they follow the methods properly. In other cases, the problem isn't technical, but will arise because the job is being done out of sequence, or without the proper background information.

2. Try to get independent advice. If you have access to an independent reviewer (for example in the QA group) then use him or her to evaluate information and explain things to you. If not, canvas opinion from other members of the team. It's important to show that this is not just checking for errors, but an important part of making sure there is a joint understanding of the situation.

3. Get the person(s) asking the question or presenting the problem to find and assess a number of options for its solution. Use risk analysis techniques (see next section) to evaluate the impact of each option on the project, then choose the option which has the greatest benefit/risk ratio.

4. Try to reduce what you are told to a form you do understand. You may be able to work by analogy, or get the members of your team to use simpler examples.

5. Ask the right questions. If you don't understand the answers, you may need to ask different questions.

The last point is probably the key. If you ask the right questions, then the answers may be obvious. My father relates the following conversation between a very bright, but blind, director of Imperial Tobacco and a telephone sales girl in a new company which had just been set up and which was to be very successful:

"Good morning my dear. You telephone the customers to get their orders?"

"Roughly how long does each call take?"

"I see, around three to five minutes."

"And you work from nine until five?"

"Can you look up on yesterday's log to see how many calls you made?"

"Twenty-five. Thank you my dear. Good morning."

Keep probing with different questions, and the answers will add up and make sense!

How Do I Spot Problems?

You have to go looking for them! If all problems announced themselves in advance with a big fanfare, then you'd just have to find a solution to each one and put it into practice at the right time. This would be a lot easier than what happens in reality, where problems tend to creep up while you're not looking, and you don't notice them until too late.

As a project manager, you have to be a bit pessimistic. You can't assume that everything will always go right - it won't! Murphy's Law is probably a bit too pessimistic, but it's not a bad basis on which to manage.

> "If anything can go wrong, it will"
> Murphy's Law

Remember as well that it's human nature for most people to hide problems when they first see them, thinking either "maybe it'll go away", or "maybe I can think of a solution to this and recover without anyone knowing".

You can't manage like this. You have to try to spot problems in advance, and make plans which will cater for them with the minimum of disruption to the project. You have to encourage your team to tell you, early, about any problems they can foresee, and in turn you should notify your managers. You won't be criticised for thinking about problems (particularly if you're also thinking about solutions at the same time), and you may even be praised for it. However, if you hide problems until they are having a serious effect, your managers and users will rightly accuse you of bad project management.

You have a couple of weapons in your armoury. The main ones we have already discussed: they are communication (with everybody, and frequently), and the use of formal reporting & interim deliverables to provide you with clear information on progress (or the lack of it).

The other thing you can do is perform a formal *Risk Analysis*: You need to ask yourself the following questions:

💣   What are the potential problems?

💣   What is the probable impact of each problem?

💣   How likely is it to occur?

💣   How can I prevent it or identify it early?

💣   What do I do if it does occur?

The best way to do this is to have a brainstorming session with the team (and/or your managers and users) to get a list of possible problems. Assess the impact and likelihood of each on a scale of 1 (low) to 10 (high), and multiply the two numbers to give you a severity rating. Then, for the most severe potential problems, develop an action plan (for prevention if possible) and an outline contingency plan (in case you can't prevent it). Give someone on the team the job of tracking any indicators you can think of, so you get the maximum warning of the need to activate the contingency plan.

The following spreadsheet shows part of such a risk analysis table:

Potential Problem	Impact	Likelihood	Severity	Tracker	Action/Contingency Plan
Insufficient disk space	3	3	9	Fred	(A) Investigate cost & lead time for upgrade
Insufficient memory	2	2	4		(No action at present)
Version 1.4 of database is too buggy	9	3	27	Joe	(A) Send Joe on early training course. (C) Use V1.3
User requirements not completed on time	8	5	40	Fred	(A) Check progress and choose best areas for phased work
Users not available for testing	6	6	36	Alice	(A) Check user plans (C) Use external testers?
Late delivery of external subsystem	9	5	45	Alice	(C) Will need to build simulator for testing
Response time inadequate	7	6	42	Joe	(A) Prototype key transactions. (C) Consider second processor

Remember this is a plan, and needs to be updated and reported against like all your other plans. The "trackers" should report the state of the indicators to you as part of their progress reports. As dangers pass, you can scale down the severity of a problem and maybe drop it off the list, but you also need to review the list regularly and see if anything new needs to be added.

Is Programming Important?

The majority of software developers start their lives in the industry as programmers. You may well be one such person. Thus it's very easy to consider programming to be the core activity of software development. It takes quite a lot of effort and self-discipline, but if you want to be a successful project manager you have to stop thinking in this code-centric fashion. Instead, you should see it as just another stage, neither more nor less important than the others. Remember that if the requirements are wrong, the best programmers in the world won't deliver anything useful, and that until it's tested, all software is unproven and therefore of little value.

As well as developing this discipline for yourself, you have to develop it in the members of your team. Most programmers are at their happiest writing code, but you need to create an environment in which the delivery of the complete package (code, documents and documented tests), to a known quality standard, is what counts, not the code alone.

Be prepared, as well, to recognise the strengths and weaknesses of your team members. If some are less good as programmers, it may advance your project more rapidly if they concentrate on non-programming tasks, leaving the code-cutting to those who are best at it. Alternatively, you may find that your best programmers are also the best testers and documenters, and you have to make sure they do their share of the documentation and testing.

To make this work you will have to elevate the importance of the documentation and testing to at least equal with the coding, and possibly higher. Nobody likes to think they are second best, and the truth is that if they are doing these other jobs they may be contributing more, not less, to the project.

You'll also have to try to make the documenting and testing jobs more rewarding. This means making sure that these jobs have well-defined objectives, and are properly planned and resourced. If you've got specialist documenters or testers, then dedicate them to the appropriate jobs but recognise the special contributions they are making.

There is one further benefit of this approach. If you have resources concentrating on documentation and testing at the same time as the coding, you're less likely to be caught in the "testing trap" with a pressing deadline and these important jobs not done.

What Do I Do?

1. As project manager, you must:

   • Lead and build the team,

   • Plan,

   • Communicate,

   • Monitor and report progress,

   • Achieve the overall project objectives.

2. A plan is only complete when for each job you can answer the questions *what?*, *why?*, *when?*, *where?*, *how?* and *who?*.

3. Talk to people, make sure they understand what they are supposed to do, and what other people are doing or expecting of them.

4. Don't confuse your project management tasks with any technical responsibilities you may have. You must dedicate some time to the management role.

5. The key aspect of leadership is to focus everyone on a common goal. Co-operation is better than coercion.

6. You don't have to give orders to get people to do things. If you understand what motivates each person, there are much better ways.

7. Don't be afraid to delegate.

8. Accept that mistakes happen. Build an environment in which there is a positive effort to find errors, correct them and prevent recurrence, but not as a criticism of the person who made the error. Submit your work to the same checks.

9. You can't force a team to "jell", but you can create the right environment by creating an open framework, avoiding defensive management and excessive paperwork and paying attention to the working environment.

10. There are a number of key roles in any team. Check your team to make sure that all the key players exist.

11.   Concentrate on making communication effective. Remember that you may need to communicate important messages in more than one way. Communicate in all directions: up to your managers, down to your team and out to the users.

12.   Learn how to sell your ideas to your managers. If you have a problem introducing the right methods, look carefully at whether your organisation is ready for such changes. If not, concentrate on the most basic good project management practices.

13.   You don't have to be an expert, as long as you can ask the right questions, and find ways of making people explain what they're telling you.

14.   Look for problems before they occur, and think of ways of preventing them, or, if all else fails, bringing in a contingency plan to limit their effect. Formal risk analysis is a very good way of doing this.

15.   Programming is not the most important activity in a software development project. You have to make sure that you expend good-quality effort on the management jobs, and on things like documentation and testing.

16.   Get a firm sign-off of each stage or interim deliverable.

The best further reading in this area is, without a doubt, *Peopleware*. *Make It So* and *Debugging the Development Process* are strong on how to direct and manage people. *The Decline and Fall of the American Programmer* and *Software Project Management* also have very strong "peopleware" sections, including good advice on how to build effective and balanced teams. The latter book goes into a lot more detail on risk analysis.

The Development Life-Cycle

It's easier to do a job if you understand what you have to do, why, and in what sequence.

In an attempt to make the job of software development easier to understand, control and repeat successfully, people have invented a variety of "methods", or "processes" based around a basic life-cycle which suggests a sequence for the main development activities.

Many methods use a variation on the basic "Waterfall" life-cycle, in which early stages define the requirements for the system. A design stage creates a physical design to meet these requirements, and subsequent stages build, test and deliver that solution. The rest of this book follows a similar structure.

The waterfall life cycle can serve as a structure for most commercial systems development. However, waterfall methods have their limitations, which you need to understand.

A "Waterfall" Method!

Other methods take a different approach, recognising that many of the development activities happen alongside one another. They aim to reduce risk by delivering the system a bit at a time (incrementally), repeating some processes over and over again for each increment (iteration). Some are quite formal, while others employ a lot less modelling and documentation.

This chapter looks at the basic waterfall life-cycle, and a method based on it. It also discusses the major alternatives, and common techniques such as prototyping. I compare the methods, and provide some guidance on where each is best used, so you can decide how to structure your development activities.

What is the Waterfall Life-Cycle?

The diagram to the right shows a typical development life-cycle. I chose it for this book because it's fairly simple, but most "waterfall" methods are based on something similar. The flow-charts might be a different shape, and there may be a different number of stages (with different names), but the underlying ideas will be quite alike.

It is important to understand the difference between *Strategy*, *Analysis* and *Design*.

At the *Strategy* stage, you must define what you are trying to achieve with the development and how you are going to achieve it. You should also define who has what responsibilities in the development. At the end of the *Strategy* stage a decision can be taken on how to proceed with the project. It's important not to invest too

```
        ┌──────────────┐
        │   STRATEGY   │
        └──────┬───────┘
               ▼
        ┌──────────────┐
        │   ANALYSIS   │
        └──────┬───────┘
               ▼
        ┌──────────────┐
        │    DESIGN    │
        └──┬────────┬──┘
           ▼        ▼
   ┌────────┐  ┌──────────────┐
   │ BUILD  │  │ DOCUMENTATION│
   └────┬───┘  └──────┬───────┘
        └──────┬───────┘
               ▼
        ┌──────────────┐
        │  TRANSITION  │
        └──────┬───────┘
               ▼
        ┌──────────────┐
        │  PRODUCTION  │
        └──────────────┘
```

A Waterfall Life-Cycle

much effort in detailed analysis (or design!) without a sound strategy, making sure everyone understands what you are proposing and agrees to it.

At the *Analysis* stage you define the requirements in detail, in terms of the business functions the user will perform with the system. You must have already defined the scope of the system in the *Strategy*, so you can limit any growth in the requirements ("scope creep"), or at least control it using change control.

At the *Design* stage you turn the business requirements into a physical design for the system. The most important thing here is not the detailed specifications for particular elements, but to make sure you have a good architecture for the system, to understand (and communicate to others) how the different parts of the system will fit together and interact.

Once you have built the system (or a defined portion of it), you need to deliver it to the users, and help them implement it. The various processes of user and integration testing, training, completion of user procedures and documentation, data take-on and so forth are lumped together into the *Transition* stage. Some methods have a separate *Testing* stage, but this model doesn't, since testing is something which should happen alongside the other activities in all the stages.

What Else Makes Up A Structured Method?

As well as defining the life-cycle, most methods then provide two other main things:

1.   They break down the stages of the life-cycle down into more detailed lists of jobs to be done within each stage, and deliverables to be produced.

2.   They suggest (or even *mandate*) a set of techniques and conventions which you should use in the main tasks of analysis and design. For example data analysis might use Entity-Relationship diagrams (drawn according to a particular set of conventions).

A particular method may be supported by one or more CASE (*Computer-Aided Systems Engineering*) tools - these usually store the analysis and design information in a central database or *repository*, provide tools for drawing the diagrams and may even partially automate the move from one stage of the life-cycle to the next. However, it's perfectly possible to use most methods without CASE tools if you don't have them.

Different methods use different techniques for analysis and design. These techniques are not interchangeable, but with care you should be able to use a particular technique within the overall structure of a method which doesn't usually employ that technique.

What Do the Different Terms Mean?

One of the biggest differences between methods is their terminology. For clarity, here's what I mean when I use certain words:

Method	An overall structure for a job, such as development, or testing. The methods for development are sometimes known as *methodologies* or *processes*.
Stage	A major division of a development method. The end of a stage usually corresponds to a shift in emphasis and the viewpoint from which the system is being defined.
Phase	A division of a system for development and delivery, often related to a major functional division of the system.
Technique	An individual mechanism that can be employed within the structure of a method, such as entity-relationship diagramming.
Task	A job that has to be done within a particular stage. In some cases, this is known as an *activity*, while other methods may use "task" and "activity" in a hierarchical relationship.

What is Missing from Most Waterfall Methods?

Most structured methods based on the waterfall life-cycle suffer from a number of limitations. Thinking about them may identify potential problems to be avoided, and ways of working around them.

"First catch your bear." Like the famous recipe for bear stew, a lot of methods start with an instruction like "look at your existing systems". This is fine if you have an existing business (which isn't expected to change much as a direct result of computerisation) or existing systems, whether computer- or paper-based.

However, you may be in the position of developing systems for a new business, or one where the existing systems are inadequate. The user managers may not yet know how they want the business to function. In this case, the act of thinking about the computer system will start to shape the way the business works. This is likely to be an iterative process, with analysis and business structure advancing together step-by-step. Even with an existing business, you may find that your work causes changes to the business which weren't intended. Most structured methods don't really cater for these problems, assuming instead that you can make a definitive assessment of the business processes at an early stage.

Legacy Systems. This is the opposite problem. You may have to either maintain or "reverse engineer" very old systems. (Reverse engineering is the process of getting back to design or analysis from an existing system for which you don't have the full documentation). The structured methods may be quite helpful in understanding and documenting what the old systems do, but they'll give you very little help in managing or maintaining the old systems while you work towards the new ones.

Tackling risks late. One of the biggest problems with waterfall methods is the way that you have no confirmation that your system will work, or even that it's the right system, until very late in the project. Some fundamental mis-understanding may result in an enormous amount of wasted work. It is much better to find a way of delivering something early, which confirms you are on the right track, proves the technical solution and proves your ability to your managers and users.

Wicked problems. Some problems don't lend themselves to solution by a classic software development. For example, it may not be clear what the right solution is, there's no easy way to test each solution and the cost of a wrong solution may be huge or permanent. A lot of safety-critical software has these constraints. Alternatively, some problems cannot be fully understood until you have found the solution - this is obviously fundamentally different to the waterfall approach. If you have problems of this sort, then you will probably need to use a different method. You may have to produce a first-cut solution to help the users understand the problem, and then be prepared for a second iteration to formalise the approach.

Phasing. There's no law which says that all of a new software system has to be delivered to the users at the same time, right at the end of development. Most structured methods assume that you're going to analyse it all, then design it all, and then build and deliver it all. It may be much better to split the work up into phases, each of which goes through the life-cycle separately.

Lack of traceability. It can be very difficult to trace the requirements through to the code, or the functions back to the requirements. Some methods try to introduce strict numbering schemes and explicit relationships to address this, while others ignore the problem and expect you to invent a solution.

Technical standards. Most methods concentrate on the early stages of development such as *Strategy* and *Analysis*. You will almost certainly have to supplement them with standards for the *Design, Build* and later stages which establish good practices for the actual implementation environment and languages you will use.

Testing. Some methods are very naive about testing, and assume it's something which you can do once you have built the software. This leaves finding errors to the end, when they're most expensive to fix! Instead, the process of testing must be fully integrated into all stages of the life-cycle, so that every deliverable must be promptly reviewed or tested in some way. Each requirement must lead directly to one or more tests of the system.

Documentation. You need to view each document as another sub-system, with its own purpose (strategy), required content (analysis) and design. However, some methods simply view the production of documentation as a "black art" not requiring such an approach.

Procurement. Some or all of the system may come from an outside supplier. You will have to ensure that he delivers what he says he will, and when he says he will. Most methods give you very little support in this area.

Many methods are the result of an attempt to reduce the skill required in development. This is intrinsically wrong - development *is* a skilled job, and instead you must use the method as a support for the application of your own skill, knowledge and common sense.

Over the next few pages, we look at alternative approaches that address these issues.

How Do Iterative and Incremental Methods Work?

The main alternative to the waterfall life-cycle is to deliver software a bit at a time (incrementally), repeating parts of the development process for each delivery cycle (iteration). Several such methods exist, most of them developed specifically to address the known problems of waterfall methods.

The diagram illustrates a typical process of this type. After some initial planning, development proceeds in a *cycle* of planning, requirements gathering and analysis, design, implementation and testing. At the end of each cycle there should be a usable release, and you then evaluate the cycle just finished, before the next one starts.

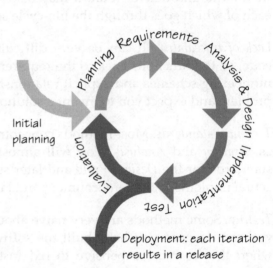

An Iterative and Incremental Process

There are a number of benefits to this:

✓ You can identify and correct serious misunderstandings early,

✓ You can identify technical and requirement risks early, when you have the most chance of controlling them,

✓ The users can use early versions of the system to refine their requirements, and their understanding of how the system will fit or change their business process,

✓ Testing becomes a continuous process, avoiding the "testing trap". Repeated testing and user involvement lead to a better quality system,

✓ Your team's workload is spread more evenly, and each person can work continuously on appropriate tasks, instead of having to switch from analysis to design and so on. This is much better for a small team with mixed skills,

✓ You and your team can learn from each cycle to improve the next one, and learn new skills gradually along the way,

✓ You are more likely to re-use software and other deliverables,

✓ Your managers and customers get early evidence of your progress.

The Rational Unified Process (RUP) is one good example of a method like this. This has an "Inception" phase for initial planning, and then a repeating cycle of Elaboration, Construction and Transition phases.

During the Inception phase you establish the business case, outline the core requirements, make an initial risk assessment and define the project's scope.

The Elaboration phase of each cycle, which can take about 20% of the time, has three important activities which usually proceed in parallel:

✍ Analysing the requirements: you should apply an "80/20" rule, targeting your effort at the problems relevant to the current cycle, and leaving difficult problems, or areas which aren't immediately relevant, to a later cycle,

✍ Defining the architecture: RUP recognises that a good architecture is vital, and that it has to be defined, and tested, early to reduce technical risks. The architecture work may include technical prototypes,

✍ Planning the construction phase. This is itself broken down into a number of smaller iterations. Your aim should be to reduce risks and deliver user benefits as early as possible (see page 64 on planning incremental development).

The Construction phase makes up most of each cycle, where you build, test and deliver the software. In a large project, the construction phase may itself be broken up into several iterations. The tasks include:

✍ Confirming the detail requirements (for a group of use cases),

✍ Changing the analysis-level models to a physical design (see page 150),

✍ Writing the code, and other "building" tasks,

✍ Testing (including user acceptance if the output is meant to be used in anger),

✍ Planning how to deliver or deploy the system to the users.

The Transition phase includes actually putting the system into use, and re-assessing the plan and risks ready for the next cycle.

You should plan each iteration in the Construction phase so that a small team (of around 3-4 full-time members) can deliver something useful in a few weeks. You may decide to use the technique of "timeboxing" so that you fix the delivery date for each cycle, and deliver what you can (this is described further in the next section).

How Does Rapid Application Development Work?

Something like the Rational Unified Process is still quite formal, with a lot of emphasis on formal planning, architecture, and reviewing documents and models. "Rapid Application Development" (RAD) methods adopt the same principles of iterative and incremental delivery, but instead focus on getting the users and developers working very closely together. The key deliverables are the code and executable system, rather than documents and models, and the system essentially grows by a process of continuous prototyping and refinement.

There are several RAD methods, but the best known are probably the *Dynamic Systems Development Method* (DSDM), and *eXtreme Programming* (XP).

DSDM is based on 9 key principles:

1. Active user involvement – users are constant participants in the development process, refining the requirements and building joint ownership of the system,

2. The team (of developers and users) is empowered to make decisions, usually without having to seek management approval,

3. The team focuses on frequent deliveries, and can therefore decide which activities are necessary to deliver the right products,

4. There's a focus on "fitness for purpose" – the system has to meet the essential business requirements with acceptable quality, anything else is a bonus,

5. Iterative and incremental development is used to converge on a solution,

6. Changes are reversible, so that it is easy to get back to a known, working, state,

7. High-level requirements are "base-lined" (frozen) to control the system's scope,

8. The system is tested continuously by both users and developers,

9. Collaboration and cooperation between all stakeholders is essential.

Instead of fixing the requirements, DSDM controls development by *timeboxing*, in which the duration of an iteration is fixed (usually 6 weeks or less), with a defined end date, and the requirements are treated as flexible. To achieve this, you classify the requirements for each iteration using the following scheme (the MoSCoW method):

✓   *Must* Have (requirements which must be satisfied in this iteration),

✓ Should Have (requirements which should be delivered, but could be omitted),

✓ Could Have (optional requirements which will be delivered if time permits),

✓ Will Not Have (known requirements which are out of scope for this iteration).

You must have some non-mandatory requirements in each timebox, otherwise you don't have enough flexibility. Good configuration control is also essential, since you have to be able to get back easily to an earlier working state. You should aim for adequate quality at each iteration, but some rework can be deferred to the next one.

Because of the close user involvement, your users should feel they "own" the system, the risk of building "the wrong system" is small, the users will be better trained, and implementation should go smoothly because all parties have been involved early.

Done this way, a RAD project can still use quite formal processes to define the high-level requirements and the system's architecture. By comparison eXtreme Programming puts programming at the heart of the process, and controls the quality and content of the system through a number of continuous review processes:

↻ Programmers work in pairs so that all code is constantly reviewed,

↻ Tests are designed before code is written, and all tests are run repeatedly,

↻ The design is continuously refined through a process of *refactoring*, restructuring the code to address identified design weaknesses,

↻ Instead of "thinking ahead" and designing for flexibility, programmers must implement the simplest solution for the current functionality,

↻ The architecture and functional structure are expressed as a metaphor, to which every team member can contribute,

↻ The system is integrated and tested continuously, at least once a day.

In other respects XP is a typical RAD process, but with very short iterations. The biggest risk is that the resulting system will have a poor architecture unable to respond to future changes, and may not be easily integrated with other systems.

📖 The best DSDM resource is www.dsdm.org. XP is described in *eXtreme Programming Explained*, and refactoring in Martin Fowler's book *Refactoring*.

What Can Go Wrong?

There are a variety of things that can go wrong in a development. Some of these are due to limitations of a particular method, but most are due to problems of communication and management, as the well-known cartoon here shows.

The users (or, worse, their managers) may be over-ambitious, either about what the system will achieve, or the functions which you can deliver within the budget, time and quality constraints. They may also be over-optimistic about the amount of change which the business processes will

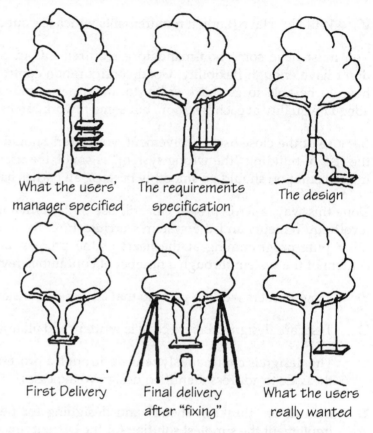

What the users' manager specified

The requirements specification

The design

First Delivery

Final delivery after "fixing"

What the users really wanted

allow, or the readiness of the users to work with new technology. You must make a lot of effort in the *early* stages (Strategy and Analysis or their equivalent) to understand and communicate how the computer system will fit into the business. Leaving it until you have something designed and built is too late. This is especially true if you are prototyping a solution, rather than doing a formal analysis.

A variation on this problem is the user who specifies the tools or technology he wants you to use, but cannot identify the business processes which will get clear benefit from automation. If you can't find any, the user doesn't need a computer system.

You must make sure you have a clear description of the requirements for the system, *in terms the user can understand*. This means stating things in terms of the business, not in terms of a computer system design.

The designer has to work from the statement of requirements and design a solution to meet them. If the analyst and architect or designer are different people, this is a common area of mis-communication, as the designer may not fully understand the requirements. Alternatively, the architect or designer may be over-ambitious, using a technology or introducing features for their own sake, rather than in response to a requirement. You should aim to choose the simplest solution consistent with the overall constraints such as the quality standards.

Similarly, the architecture and design must be communicated to the programmers. If the design is poorly documented (or poorly structured) then further misunderstandings will occur. Unless they are controlled, the programmers may stray from the design or introduce unnecessary complexity.

If the requirements are constantly changing, any development can be overwhelmed by the weight and frequency of the changes, and will go rapidly out of control. Changes to the requirements (or to the environment in which the system must operate) must be applied to the analysis, and then cascaded through to the design and the code in some controlled fashion. If is uncontrolled, then everyone is trying to hit a moving target. In a badly-managed project, the programmers may directly implement the changes, leaving the analysis and design documents unchanged, and out-of-date, but no-one will know what has happened. This is much worse!

Each stage of the process will introduce errors. If these errors are "fixed" by fixing-up the latest stage of work with no reference to the deliverables from the earlier stages, the final system will rapidly become a patchwork of fixes with no firm foundation. Instead, if you detect an error when showing part of the system to a user, make sure that the user's requirement is consistent with what you analysed. If it is consistent, try to find out where the requirement became mis-translated. If not, then you must handle this as a proper change, and apply it to the analysis and design first.

Projects run under structured methods can fail if there is too little paperwork, with things not properly written down and communicated. However, they can also fail with too *much* paperwork: no-one can read and verify shelf-feet of documentation, and it can become impossible to maintain. There is no one right solution to this; *you* must make the decision, but the answer is not "none" or "tons".

Development sometimes seems to be a massive game of Chinese whispers, with the requirements being translated into forms more and more difficult for the users to understand. You will have to dedicate quite a lot of effort to *communicating* at each stage, and making sure that the users understand and agree with what you are saying. You must also look for opportunities to *check* the work, for example by involving the architect or analyst in the design review and *vice-versa*.

How Do I Choose A Method?

You may not have a choice! Your organisation, or your customer, may specify that you have to follow a particular method. If so, you must make sure you understand the method thoroughly, and know what is expected from you and others at each stage.

If you have a choice, or if you need to challenge an imposed method, the starting point is to consider the different risks in your project, and how to address them.

Waterfall methods are very good where the technology and tools are well understood, and the requirements can be clearly defined before the software is built. You may be able to exploit previous experience and measurements to produce good estimates, and the scope of the system at delivery will be well defined. Alternatively, if the cost of testing and delivering new versions of the system is likely to be very high, you may have to use a waterfall method (or an incremental method with very few iterations).

Waterfall methods work badly where there is significant novelty or risk. They are unsuitable if the tools and technologies are unknown, there are known technical risks, or the requirements are unclear or constantly changing. Large-scale iterative and incremental methods such as RUP directly address these risks, but retain sufficient formality that they can be used on large and complex projects or in quite formal contractual situations. This sort of method is also the best choice if you are building a large system using object and component technologies. You can tailor RUP in particular to fit a range of project situations, making it a good general-purpose choice. However, it does rely on strong skills in analysis and design, and on users who know what they want.

RAD methods may be a good choice where the requirements are very uncertain, and the challenge is to deliver *something* quickly, or where you have a team with good development skills but poor formal analysis, design and documentation skills. These methods can be used as long as the team can be kept quite small, with good, continuous user involvement, and someone to keep control of the architecture, design and plans.

RAD methods will not work if you have insufficient user participation, or management refuse to empower the team to make decisions. Other warning signs are where frequent deliveries will be costly or difficult, the quality constraints are strong, or the architecture is very complex. As a general rule, RAD methods are not suited to large projects (with teams of more than about 10 people), or to projects with a high cost of failure (such as "mission-critical" systems).

How Do I Use the Method?

Remember: the method is there to serve you. Use it to create a structure for your work to communicate to your users, managers and team. It will define what jobs have to be done, in which order, and may define the deliverables you have to produce at each stage. All this is very useful, provided you apply a bit of common sense.

You may be able to use the method to help you formalise your plans. Certainly your plans should be in terms of the stages and tasks given by the method. However, you may decide to split the development up into phases in a way that the method doesn't automatically support, and here you will have to apply some ingenuity.

You will have to make some decisions about the techniques you will adopt. In some cases, you will want to add techniques not normally supported. For example, you may wish to do some prototyping in a method which isn't a "prototyping" method, or you may want to use a different diagramming technique. Other methods employ a large number of techniques, and you will have to choose which ones are most appropriate for your project.

While some methods are a bit over-prescriptive and imply that you don't have this freedom, most have an early "quality planning" stage where you make and formalise such decisions. The important thing is to make any such decisions early, document them properly in your Quality Plan, and get agreement from your managers and users.

Don't try to use too many analysis or diagramming techniques: they will impose an extra load on your team (and your users if you want them to understand your work). Typically, the analysis has three "degrees of freedom": for example the functions provided to the user, the static data structure and the dynamic way in which the data changes with time. A good rule of thumb is therefore to choose three techniques, each of which concentrates on one of these aspects. I'll discuss this further later in the book.

Remember that a method is a means to an end, not an end in itself. Don't use it as a crutch or a prison! *You* have to apply your common sense and make sure that the method serves you and your objectives.

How do I Control Changes?

In a game of football, it's very difficult to score if the goalposts are moving. In the same way, the "moving goalposts" of uncontrolled changes can spoil your project.

The users may generate a stream of changes to the requirements, even after you have agreed the requirement specification. If you attempt to address each one as it arrives, it will generate confusion, and you will dissipate much of your development effort in trying to understand the constantly-changing situation. Conflicting changes will waste effort as people undo what someone else has done. If there is always "one more change" then you will never deliver. Too many user changes may mean you have to go back and do some more analysis.

However, not all changes come from the users. You may find that your managers change the time or budget constraints under which you are working - if these are impractical don't be afraid to say so. Other developers may change interfaces, or the environment in which the system runs. Your own developers may seek to change the design, or to introduce features which weren't planned. Worst of all, you may try to do any or all of these things yourself in response to user comments, fears of project slippage or concerns about errors (see "What if People Make Mistakes?" on page 28).

You *have* to exert control over changes. You don't have any choice. This requires discipline and a certain amount of assertiveness ("I *won't* do that till the next release"), but is absolutely essential if you want your project to succeed. There are a few simple principles for change control:

- Make sure *every* proposed change is written down and the record kept in some central place. Make it clear that verbal requests aren't worth the paper they are (or should that be *aren't?*) written on, and you will treat them as such.

- Evaluate each change request. It may be due to a mis-understanding, or it might be completely impractical. Make sure you understand the *business reason* for changes - "I would like..." isn't a good enough reason for a major change.

- Agree on a priority for the change. Make it quite clear that you won't treat all requests as "top priority". If your users can't do this, then reduce it to simple arguments like "I can either do the urgent, urgent change you gave me yesterday, or this urgent, urgent change. Please choose one of them!".

- Check, and communicate, the impact of the change. Make sure you understand the impact of the change on the analysis, the design and the tests, as well as the code. You may need the help of your analysts, designers and testers to do this.

- Plan the change. Batch changes up into groups and make them together. Make sure you include updating all affected documents. Don't be afraid of saying "this change will go into the batch I'll tackle next month."

- Communicate to your team, your users, your managers and anyone else who might be affected, which changes will be made and when. Then make sure that you track the progress of the change against your plan for it.

If you have an existing change control system, *use* it. If not, don't try to invent anything too complex, but keep a simple, central written record of all change requests and what you do with each of them.

You will find it difficult to control changes if your users, or, worse, your managers, don't understand the problems. The most important thing to do is *talk* to them, but there are a few simple defensive actions you can take:

✓ Write everything down ("to make sure I've understood").

✓ Get a firm sign-off of each stage or interim deliverable. You then have a clear baseline against which something is either a change, or not.

✓ Plan your changes and communicate the plans. If the "changers" can see that you've got control, they may well come around to your way of working.

Try to allow for a certain amount of change. If you think a value or a rule may change, make sure the design allows it to be changed easily (ideally in the data). Concentrate on creating a modular design which is flexible and extensible (there's more on this in the "Design" chapter). Keep your documents short and well-targeted so that you can change them with the minimum of fuss.

When you come to implement a change, *change the analysis document and the test materials first* before attempting to change the design, and finally the code. If you can't do this easily, then you don't understand the change. If that's the case, discuss the change and seek clarification before doing anything else.

What is the Role of Prototyping?

Even if your chosen development method is not a "prototyping" method, prototypes may be of use in development, for example:

➡ Early (analysis) prototypes may help to clarify the understanding of the users' requirements. It is often easier to discuss some physical representation of a problem rather than an abstract one. However, do not allow this to degenerate into progressive "enhancements" to an undocumented core.

➡ Analysis prototypes may help to demonstrate and assess user reaction to issues such as screen design.

➡ Design prototypes may be useful in establishing whether a proposed technical solution is, in fact, viable.

➡ In some cases, you will need to use an intermediate solution to investigate the problem and confirm the requirements for the final solution, and also to support the business while you complete the development. You might derive this intermediate solution from a prototype, a legacy system, or an externally procured package.

Prototyping is useful as an intermediate step within a formal development, but you must *always* formally document the requirements for the replacement system. There are three main dangers of a prototype or intermediate solution:

1. The temporary solution will never be replaced, and future maintainers will have to struggle to maintain a sub-standard and undocumented system.

2. The temporary solution will establish prejudices about how the final solution should work, or the technology which will be used.

3. Documentation and testing work will be more difficult if the development isn't properly documented at the right time.

4. Users may think the project's nearly finished, when there's a lot of work left.

Make sure that you properly document and approve the development, whether you have used prototypes or not. These formal documents should be the basis of future work, with the prototype as a backup, rather than a prime source of detailed information. If at all possible, you should insist that prototypes are "thrown away", and not used against live data.

How Should I Structure My Project?

1. It's easier to understand your job if it has a structure, so you know what you have to do, why and in what sequence. Most commercial developments can be structured a "waterfall" life-cycle or an iterative and incremental one.

2. If your organisation has a preferred method for software development, use it. If not, choose one matched to your team's skills and the project's risks. Within a method, you will need to make decisions about which tools and techniques are appropriate to your job, and document this in an agreed Quality Plan.

3. You must understand the limitations of your method so you can spot and plan for potential problems. Even if the method and project match well, various things can go wrong, due mainly to communication problems. Be aware of these and work to avoid them.

4. Understand the role of prototypes and intermediate solutions. They can be very useful, but you must be careful not to let them lead you into an undocumented and uncontrolled development on shaky foundations.

5. Make sure you understand the principles of change control. If your organisation has an existing change control method, use it. If not, follow some simple guidelines, the most important of which is to make sure that *all* changes are written down. *You* must control the changes.

6. At the end of the day, any method is only a guideline. Don't allow yourself to be imprisoned by it. Use your "little grey cells", rather than looking on the method as a magic recipe.

The next chapter, "Structuring the Development" builds on the ideas discussed here, and considers how to divide up the work, and how to make best use of your resources to do that work.

📕   The best description of different methods, their strengths and their limitations is probably in *Wicked Problems, Righteous Solutions*. *The Decline and Fall of the American Programmer* contains a similar, if briefer, discussion. The best advice on change and configuration control is probably in *Software Configuration Management*, but there's also a good section in *Software Project Management* and some of the other books.

Structuring the Development

In any development there are a large number of jobs to be done and deliverables to be completed. You may have several people, each of whom have different skills. Before you can produce a detailed plan, think how you are going to structure the work and your team.

There are three main ways to divide up the work and the team:

1. *By functional area*. Divide the work in line with the major functional divisions of the system, and give a small team (or individual) responsibility for each one. For example, one group might build the investments sub-system and another the loans sub-system.

2. *By activity*. Get part of your team to concentrate on analysis, part on design, part on build and so forth. Each sub-team will perform the same work for all the functional areas. For example, your analysts will analyse the investments sub-system, and then move onto loans once investments has been handed over to the designers.

3. *By technical specialisation and design*. Assign technical specialists to particular tasks, and divide the design and build effort according to the structure of the design itself. For example, the database will be designed and built by your database expert, and the user interface will be designed by someone else.

These are not mutually exclusive, and you will probably employ all three approaches to some extent. How you divide the work will affect how you describe the system and *vice-versa*. Think as well about how to maintain control in both management and technical terms. The rest of this chapter discusses the options open to you, and provides guidelines on structuring your own project.

How Do I Divide Up a Development?

Your project structure will need to achieve a number of things:

☺ Create clear boundaries to the job done by each individual or sub-team.

☺ Assign deliverables clearly to one individual or sub-team.

☺ Match the content of work packages to the skills of the assigned team members.

How you describe the project will affect your team structure, since you may want to assign a discrete part of the project to an individual or sub-team. During a project's life, there will typically be three descriptions of the project:

1. *Functional decomposition.* Derived from the high-level analysis, the most obvious division is into the main sub-sets of the functions you must provide. These may align themselves naturally with different groups of users, or with different target schedules for the system's introduction.

2. *Design decomposition.* The high-level design may suggest a division of labour with, for example, different groups working on the front-end and the database.

3. *Work breakdown structure.* This is the complete list of jobs you must do to take the project through to conclusion. The main divisions will be the stages of the life-cycle, possibly with subdivision by function or design.

These may be different, but there will be a strong relationship between them. The following sections discuss how you may use each to structure the development.

Dividing by Functional Area

This is a natural division, since it allows an individual or small sub-team to concentrate on the details of one set of functions, and the needs of one group of users. However, if all the functions must be delivered together, then splitting your development like this has a major disadvantage. Each team must have a reasonable level of expertise in all the main development tasks, so it must contain a good analyst, a good designer and so on. If you have only one person with each skill then they will have to split their time between jobs, which may be difficult to manage. Also, the teams will have to liaise, and it may be difficult to keep the standards and designs consistent between the sub-systems. If the total size of your team is small, it may be better to find a structure which allows people with particular skills to specialise.

If you can deliver the functions at different times, this type of division may be more useful. You can still make use of your specialists, but they can work on each functional division in turn. Effectively, you will split the total delivery into "phases". Phased development is discussed in more detail in the next section.

Dividing by Design Structure

Many developments split naturally after you have started the design into sections based on the design itself. For example, it may be sensible to give one programmer the job of building the database and another the front-end screens. If you can arrange this, it can be of great benefit. You can direct specialist skills where they are most effective, and improve the likelihood of clean, simple interfaces between the different parts of the structure. However, to do this you have to have a good, modular overall design into which the various components fit, and you do have to insist on properly documented interfaces between the levels.

This sort of approach comes easily out of the most modern client-server databases and object-oriented development methods, and may in fact be essential for these. Consider the currently popular model of a client-server application:

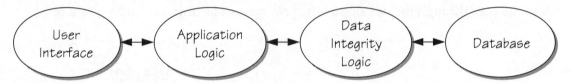

There's a natural division here (particularly if the database and data integrity logic are on a different platform to the rest). Take advantage of this, and insist that the application designers can only access the database via the interface defined by the database designers, and you immediately have a more modular structure.

A Hybrid Approach, and the Need for Change

You will probably end up with a hybrid approach such as specialists working on particular areas (like testing, documentation and overall design), but several small application build teams (with their analysts) split functionally.

Obviously you can't set this structure up from day one - you won't know the functional division at that point, and there will be further changes when you know the impact of the design. The most important thing is to keep the roles and deliverables clear, so that if the structure has to change you can change it with the minimum of problems.

How Do I Split the Project into Phases/Iterations?

If you are following an iterative and incremental method, then one of your key tasks is to plan the iterations, deciding what functionality goes into each, how it is resourced, and the scope or timebox which limits it.

However, even with a waterfall method you may be unable to fully define all the requirements for a system before starting to build it, if:

✗   The business is changing very rapidly (for example, just starting from scratch),

✗   There is considerable uncertainty around an area of the requirements,

✗   The scope of the system is so large that you can't possibly understand it all.

If these are true, then by the time analysis is complete the business will have moved on and the requirements will no longer be current. Alternatively, the users may indicate that you should deliver some parts of the system later than others. It may be best to divide the work up into a number of "Phases", each of which moves most or all of the way through the development cycle before starting on a subsequent one:

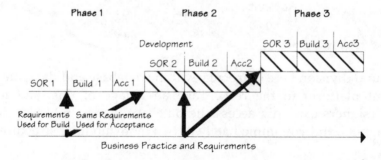

The above diagram represents such a phased structure. You define a Statement of Requirements (SOR) for a phase, and perform development and testing against those requirements. You can then create a new SOR, including some or all of the deferred requirements, and reflecting the up-to-date understanding of the business.

Phased or incremental development is not without risks, and the developers and users must act responsibly for it to be a success:

✎   The quality of the system (whether developed from scratch or based on a "package") must be high enough that later developments can build on the basis of earlier Phases. You must carefully plan for re-use, and a good, modular, documented design is a pre-requisite.

- Follow good change control practices at all times, so that the boundaries between phases do not become blurred, and the number of phases and minor redeliveries is not too great.

- The users must fully understand the structuring of functions into phases, and must be careful to test and accept systems against the agreed requirements for that phase, not the latest understanding of the changing business.

- The overall requirements must be understood well enough before the first build so that the design can support later phases, and the budget is predictable. The biggest risk is that the detailed estimates for later phases will bear little relation to the earlier outline estimates. Conversely, it may be easier to justify new expenditure on the basis of proven progress and benefit.

So Which Parts Do I Deliver First?

Don't aim to deliver the greatest possible functionality for a given budget. You will always use the full budget, and usually exceed it. You may get trapped delivering complex functions when something simpler would do. Instead, aim to deliver the simplest things of real business benefit first. That way, the user sees real benefit, and you can constrain the highest costs later, if necessary, without losing that benefit. Psychologically this works to your advantage, since you can often deliver something useful early, to prove that the development is going well. Simply put, the principle is:

$$\boxed{\text{Lowest Cost, Simplest First!}}$$

When assessing which elements to put into which phases, or the build order within a phase, evaluate the value of each item using the following equation:

$$\boxed{\text{Value} = \text{Benefit} / (\text{Cost} * \text{Risk})}$$

Plan to deliver the items in descending order of "Value" (or as near as possible subject to practical precedence constraints). A simple estimate of benefit, cost and risk (e.g. technical complexity) on a scale of 1 to 5 is often enough.

It should be obvious that you can maximise the delivered value to the users at any given point in time by this simple strategy. Items of high cost or risk will tend to follow the easier ones.

What are My Options for Team Structure?

When you've got the members of your team together, and have decided how to divide up the work, you need to decide on a team structure. This will let people do their allotted work but allow you to keep control of the various aspects of the development (progress, changes, conformance to the design, quality and so on).

You need to create this structure for several reasons:

❖ When too many people attempt to work closely together, the lines of communication become confused. I suggest that the maximum number of people who can work on the same task is two or three. Thus you will have to sub-divide a large team.

❖ You will want to assign tasks and deliverables to particular groups or individuals, and know the primary task of any group or individual at any time. If you don't make this assignment, you will find that some jobs that are a "collective responsibility" never get tackled. Alternatively, if a group's efforts are fragmented between too many tasks then those which are perceived as a lower priority will remain undone.

❖ It helps quality and management to create a supplier-customer relationship between the groups and individuals within your team. Each deliverable is produced *by* someone, *for* someone else, which helps in targeting deliverables as discussed in the first chapter. By creating this relationship, if one member produces unacceptable deliverables the others will not feel pressured into quietly correcting his deliverables, but will help him to correct them himself.

However, beware! This change of developer viewpoint from supplier to customer across sub-system boundaries does not always come naturally. It is something you will have to explain and actively encourage.

There are a number of established team structures, which differ mainly in the way that technical and managerial leadership are assigned:

☞ *The democratic team.* You function as a co-ordinator, administering and representing the team, but you take most decisions collectively. If you have a small and relatively experienced team then this may work well. It is probably unsuitable if your team is very large, has a very mixed composition, or is mainly very junior developers, in which cases clear leadership is necessary. It can also be difficult to maintain standards and a design within this structure.

☞ *The Chief Engineer team.* In this structure, you will provide both administrative and technical leadership. You will have to provide clear technical direction and supervise the members of the team. This is a good choice if you are the most senior team member in both managerial and technical terms. If you are relying on other team members for technical direction then try another structure.

☞ *The Programmer/Copilot Team.* If you *are* providing the technical lead, you may want to share the load of your other tasks. Find a "number two" who can second you on technical issues, and take the bulk of the work of communicating the design and representing the team externally. You may also want to off-load some of the administrative load to another team member (but see below).

☞ *Matrix Management.* If you have strong management skills, but another member of the team is stronger technically, you may want to give him the job of technical supervision, while you plan and co-ordinate. This can work well, but the two of you must work very closely together, clearly dividing your responsibilities, and have an indisputable rule on who should have overall control (you!). Otherwise, the danger is that you may give conflicting messages to the other team members. The role of technical supervisor is often referred to as "the architect" or "lead designer".

The ideal solution for your team may be some combination of the above. There's no rule which says that you have to do all the administrative work yourself: if you're one of the better technical resources then by all means allocate some of the admin. to another team member but remember: *this doesn't remove from you your prime responsibilities of leadership, communication and making sure the work (including the admin.) gets done.*

If you have to create sub-teams, then they too will need structure and leadership. Any of the above models can apply, but it will probably be less formal than for your team as a whole. You may not need to do this at all for a smaller project.

Make the team structure clear as early as possible, but don't impose the structure too rigidly. Allow it to adapt to changing circumstances, but remember that you still have to discharge your responsibilities.

📖 The best discussion of team structures is probably in the classic *The Mythical Man Month. Software Project Management, Peopleware* and *Debugging the Development Process* contain some other useful ideas.

What Jobs Must be Done?

You document your decisions about the structure of the project in two places:

- The *Quality Plan* documents decisions about the overall approach to development, the team structure and the responsibilities of individuals within the team. It will also state or define the procedures you must follow to gain approval or to change these things. (See page 102 for more details.)

- The *Work Breakdown Structure* (WBS) will list the individual tasks to be performed, probably in some sort of hierarchy following the overall structure of the project life-cycle. Each task should be uniquely identified. The WBS may appear as a separate document to get approval on the structure, but it will then become an integral part of the project plan (on which you will base it).

The following is an example of part of a WBS:

Task ID	Description
3	Design
3.1	Database Design
3.2	Screen Design Standards
3.3	Program Specifications
3.3.1	Client Detail Input
3.3.2	Policy Input
3.3.3	Claim Printout
4	Build
4.1	Client Detail Input
4.2	Policy Input
4.3	Claim Printout
5	Testing
5.1	Definition of Test Scenarios for System Testing

As you can see, if you make this a spreadsheet (or use your project management tool) it can easily evolve into the full plan. The latter (or a good word-processor) should manage the numbering and indentation for you.

All work must appear in the WBS. It should include all the managerial, administrative and quality-related tasks. It should also include tasks to be performed by people outside your immediate team, since you will need to monitor them against the plan so that your own progress is not compromised.

The following is a checklist of jobs which should appear, explicitly, somewhere in your WBS. It excludes the "obvious" ones like analysis, design and coding:

☑ Planning and task assignment

☑ Progress checks on assigned tasks

☑ Regular update of plans and preparation of progress reports; regular project meetings and briefings to the users and managers

☑ Risk analysis and risk management

☑ Staffing and personnel management

☑ General administration (e.g. holiday forms & timesheets, small requisitions)

☑ Tool choice, procurement and maintenance

☑ Establishment of standards and methods

☑ Configuration management and change control administration

☑ Procurement: including preparation and issue of ITT, vendor selection, drafting and agreeing contract, vendor supervision

☑ Testing: including definition of test approach, selection of cases, documentation of cases, preparation of test data

☑ Rework and retesting following each testing stage

☑ Formal unit testing separate from ad-hoc testing during coding

☑ Integration and system testing

☑ Documentation: including definition of requirements, drafting, review, redraft, publishing, distribution

☑ Potential review and redraft of all documentary deliverables

☑ Installation and support during early use

☑ Training: including definition of purpose, preparation of materials

☑ Quality assurance: checks on performance of all the above tasks

How Do I Structure Testing?

One of the most important decisions to make, because it has a direct effect on software quality, is how to organise the testing and integration of the software. Like other key aspects of the development, you must decide, document and get this agreed at an early stage. You may be constrained by the organisation in which you work, or the methods you follow, or you may have considerable freedom in how you organise this.

A basic principle is that *no-one should be the sole (or even main) tester of their own work.* Independent testers find more errors: the creator of a piece of work has a psychological investment in it, and may be blind to its faults. Also, by keeping test and build effort separate you can start properly planned and resourced testing at an early stage of development (see page 88 for more discussion of this).

If you can, create a separate group within your team who test the components and systems once they have been built (and the builders have done sufficient testing of their own to convince themselves that the product is ready for formal testing).

There is one disadvantage of this approach: the builders may get into a habit of putting any old rubbish together and "throwing it over the fence" for the testers to sort out. To avoid this, you must do two things: keep error fixing as the responsibility of the builders (so they have more work to do if the build quality is poor); and set error targets. These are target numbers of errors found by the testers (per delivery, or per 1000 lines of code): the testers aim to find more errors than the target, while the builders aim to prevent the errors. If these targets and the test results are public, both teams will strive to improve their performance. Again, measurement and quantitative goals will help you to solve a problem. Obviously, you will have to refine the targets over time to keep both groups challenged.

You may also decide to keep the documenters and the integrators (who put the components together into the systems) separate from the builders of individual modules. This gives you some useful independence (which will improve quality), but be careful that this doesn't lead to "blame passing" when something goes wrong.

All this helps you to achieve *verification* that the system conforms to its specifications. However, none of it helps with *validation* - checking that the system is what the users need. The only way to do this is to schedule and *use* reviews to look for errors in the specification and related documentation.

OK, So What Do I Have to Do?

1. Decide how to split up the development into tasks which can be planned and tracked. Do this on the basis of the major functions, the structure of the design, the stages of the method, or a combination of these approaches.

2. You must maintain control in management terms. This means finding a structure in which each group or individual has a clear set of tasks to discharge, and every task is the responsibility of one group or person.

3. Match the content of work packages to the team members assigned to perform them.

4. Dividing by functional area is quite natural, but may have problems if you don't have enough of certain skills to go round.

5. Dividing the work in line with the design structure will allow a much closer match of tasks and skills.

6. A hybrid approach is most likely to succeed. The structure will mature as you know more about the functions and design of the system.

7. In some circumstances, it is a good idea to split the work up into phases, to be delivered at different times. There are considerable benefits from this, but be aware of the risks and work to avoid them.

8. When choosing what to deliver first, apply the simple rule "Lowest Cost, Simplest First". This will maximise the benefit to the users, and minimise the costs and risk of your development.

9. There are a number of options for team structure. Think carefully about what you are trying to achieve, and who will provide the technical and managerial leadership on your project (they need not both come from the same person). Choose a team structure and decision-making approach which seems best suited, but be prepared for it to change over time or if it doesn't work.

10. The structure of the project is documented in the Quality Plan and in the Work Breakdown Structure. There is a checklist of things to include in the WBS.

11. Think about how to arrange testing and related activities. If you can get some measure of independence into testing, it will considerably improve the software quality.

Planning and Estimating

Planning, even though it might seem a bore, is critical to the success of any project.

If you don't plan, you will never know if you are on target or not. A plan is not a piece of paper produced for your management; it is to help *you* do your job. A project plan should be an extension of the Quality Plan and part of your contract with the users to deliver.

"...Not Bad, but I think you need a bit more detail right here!"

All the tasks might seem clear at the beginning, but by the middle of the project it's easy to lose your way. A project plan should be like a road map, to help you find the signposts to the end of the project, and to make successful deliveries of software.

By understanding the principles of planning, which are quite simple, you can build on the work you have done to structure the project, and put estimates and responsibilities against each task. While there is no crystal ball to check your estimates, there are good rules of thumb which will tell you if you're about right.

You can then monitor your progress against the plan. If you think there is any danger of slippage the plan equips you to react quickly but in a controlled and sensible way.

What are the Principles of Planning?

The scope of your project and the different roles and responsibilities should be clearly defined in the Strategy Report and Quality Plan. Build on this to create a work breakdown structure (detailed task list). Don't forget to include all the supporting tasks listed on page 68. Then estimate the effort required and the duration for each task. Allocate the tasks to resources (making sure that people aren't overloaded with too much work at once) and you have a plan.

Don't plan on the basis that everything will go right. Plan for things going wrong, because they will! Make sure your plan includes any preventative work suggested by your risk analysis, and add some contingency onto the overall timescales and resourcing you need. A good estimate for general development is 20%, but discuss this with your managers and anyone else who may have some relevant experience.

Make your estimates realistic - if you know that a task takes 20 days don't reduce it to 10 to humour the users or your manager. Always discuss your estimates with your colleagues and managers; they should have some ideas to help you. It's important that the people who will actually do the work believe in the estimates for their work. If possible, get them to check your estimates. Don't create artificial deadlines in order to force them to work harder: this never works and is usually counter-productive.

When you convert effort (in man-days) into elapsed time, think about the non-project time most people have to spend: administrative jobs like timesheets, company meetings and sick days won't go away just because you haven't allowed for them. Assume four productive days a week and you'll be about right.

If you are linking your system to others don't forget to include the definition, creation and testing of the interfaces. Treat the other project teams like suppliers, whose work has to be monitored against *their* part in *your* plans.

When you have your plan, get it agreed by your users and managers. Then *use* it to communicate and to monitor progress. Update and re-issue it on a regular basis.

What level of detail do I need?

Make sure that the plan is in sufficient detail for everyone to understand what the tasks are. One line saying "implementation" is probably insufficient; you need to clearly identify the tasks. Don't forget to add in time for management of the project and for producing all the things that programmers dislike - testing, documentation and training material. Remember, all these tasks should be part of the overall plan.

Each task should have a clearly identified start and end date, with the people who will do the work also shown. This is particularly important where many activities need to occur simultaneously in short timescales.

Your plan should not only show the effort of your project team, but also the time you require from the users, other project teams, support services and vendors. They too have to plan their time: if you don't produce a plan telling users *when* and *how much* time you want, don't expect it to be miraculously available when *you* decide you want it. You may, however, exclude this effort from the total cost of the project - ask your managers how they want it shown.

You may have to include plans or estimate for other things than just people and jobs. Examples include things like hardware usage and system performance. You can apply exactly the same principles to these plans as well.

A good plan should answer the six key questions *what? why? when? where? how?* and *who?* for every task.

OK, so I've got a plan. How can I use it?

To assist your communication with your managers, team and users. The plan should help you identify the following:

- the timescales and deliverables from the project,

- what resources you have used and what resources you need to complete the project at any given time,

- tasks where your estimates were inaccurate - this will help you refine your estimates in future plans.

It should clearly show timescales, deadlines, dependencies between tasks and deliverables, so you can see when timescales are slipping and things are going wrong. Use it as the basis of individual plans for the rest of the team, enabling them to assess their own performance.

The principle is exactly the same for a new project, and for maintenance and enhancements. The level of detail for enhancements could depend on whether the enhancement is a major one or not. (You should consider anything over 10 days as a major enhancement and produce a separate small plan.)

How Do I Complete My Plan?

Once you've got the list of tasks and have estimated the effort required, convert this into a plan with projected start and end dates for each task. The following approach should help you to do this:

a.   Review the resources you have at your disposal:

   ☛ *People*. These might be specific people, or a type of person (e.g. "an analyst"). Remember that people with the same title may not have the same skills or productivity: you will have to assume the worst case unless you know them.

   ☛ *Equipment* such as a computer or a training room. Completion of your task might be impossible without these.

   ☛ *Money*. You may have a budget for more resources if you need them.

   If you have insufficient resources, or if you have not yet agreed the resourcing for your project, then discuss the likely level with your managers, based on the total estimated effort. You may have to review the resource level if the plan (from the following procedure) doesn't meet the required timescale.

b.   Work out the most logical sequence of events. There may be dependencies between different tasks, or overall constraints: write these into the plan and make sure you observe them. (This is where a project management tool, or at least a spreadsheet, is very useful.)

   Look at breaking the work up into phases, and delivering the simplest items first (see page 64 for further details). This will not only build the confidence of the team but also help you to assess the strengths and weaknesses of your team for the later more difficult phases.

c.   Assign resources to the different tasks and work out an elapsed time for each task. You should get four effective days per week, but you need to take things like holidays into account. If people are working on other projects check that they will be available for the amount of time you want, when you want them. Discuss this with other project managers and the individuals concerned.

d.   Now schedule the tasks. Set the start date of each task to the finish date of the one before it in sequence. Try changing the order and the resources allocated, subject to the constraints from steps a-c (and with no-one working more than four days/week).

Try to get maximum flexibility and yet still meet your target dates. You'll probably find that there is one chain of tasks which start right after one another with no slack between them: this is the *critical path*. If you can do anything to shorten the tasks on this path, it will shorten the whole job. Conversely, any delay will affect the whole project, so monitor these critical tasks extra carefully.

e.   Discuss and agree the project plan with your team, your managers and your users. If it does not meet the required timescales then you will have to either reduce the scope of the work, break it into phases, or find extra resources.

Consider, as an example, the following very simple Work Breakdown Structure:

Task	Description	Estimated Effort (Man-Days)
1	Strategy	4
2	Analysis	8
3	Design	4
4	Build	
4.1	Data Entry Screen	4
4.2	Reports	8
4.3	End of Month Processing	6
5	Testing	
5.1	Preparation of Test Cases	6
5.2	Running Tests, fixing & retest	6
6	Delivery	4

You have a team of three: You (Self), Andy and Bill. You will do the Strategy, Bill should do the Design, and you can split the other jobs. Work will start on 1st January. The completed plan might look like the following. (This is a very simple spreadsheet. The start formulas just copy a date from the *end* column. The end formulas take the start date, and add either *effort*7/4* or *effort*7/8*, depending on how many are assigned. I've manually picked out the critical path with a * in the *CP* column.)

Task	Description	Effort	Depends on	Who	Start	End	CP
1	Strategy	4		Self	01-Jan	08-Jan	*
2	Analysis	8	1	Self, Andy	08-Jan	15-Jan	*
3	Design	4	2	Bill	15-Jan	22-Jan	*
4	Build						
4.1	Data Entry Screen	4	3	Self	29-Jan	05-Feb	
4.2	Reports	8	3	Self, Andy	22-Jan	29-Jan	*
4.3	End of Month Processing	6	3	Bill	22-Jan	01-Feb	
5	Testing						
5.1	Preparation of Test Cases	6	2	Self, Andy	15-Jan	20-Jan	
5.2	Running Tests, fixing & retest	6	4	Andy	29-Jan	08-Feb	*
6	Delivery	4	5.2	Self, Andy	08-Feb	12-Feb	*

How Do I Plan the Staffing of the Project?

Look at the example on the previous page: you start the project, then Andy joins a bit later, and Bill later still. The three of you work together through the bulk of the project, but you can release Bill two weeks before the end. This is quite typical of most development projects: you start with a few people with management and analysis skills, increase the team by adding designers, programmers, testers and writers during the central stages, and then reduce the team again (eventually to a few managers and maintainers) at the end:

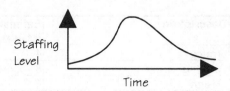

But how "long" and "thick" can you make the project? You can't bring in an infinite number of programmers and expect the coding to happen in zero time - the confusion (from too many lines of communication), learning curves and management difficulties would prevent it. On the other hand, even if you have all the skills you need, you won't do a 20 man-year project on your own!

Firstly, consider the constraints: deadlines, and any indication you may have of the maximum staffing your managers will allow. Then check that these are compatible with your estimates of total effort:

> (Maximum number of staff) x (Duration) x ½ ≥ (Estimated total effort)

(The ½ is a very crude approximation for the shape of the staffing curve.) If this equation isn't true (by a comfortable margin), then you have incompatible constraints, and need to argue for either greater staffing or longer deadlines.

Having checked this, consider how many people can work together on the tasks during the Design and Build stages of the project. Some tasks are fundamentally indivisible or incompressible: having a baby takes 9 months and one woman! Similarly, parts of the design will have to be the work of one person, to make sure the structure is coherent. You can't divide the programming tasks up beyond the point where one person is responsible for each module. But there's nothing to stop you having a couple of people planning the testing during the Design stage, and concentrating on testing during the build, for example. In fact, this is highly desirable (see "What is the "Testing Trap"?" on page 88).

When you've worked out the number of simultaneous tasks during each stage, specify the set of resources you want (in terms of managerial and technical skills), and a start date for productive work on your project. (See also "How Do I Make Sure the Team is Complete?" on page 30.)

However, this is the ideal staffing profile, and you will have to modify it to take account of two factors: learning curves, and the fact that people with the ideal skills may not be available. The first day of productive work is unlikely to be the day they are first assigned to your project.

In an ideal world, you'd have people with the right skills available when you need them, so you could bring them onto the project at exactly the right time and release them when finished. However, in the real world, you probably won't have this freedom. Your managers may assign people to your project on a basis of availability rather than suitability. Even if you are recruiting new or temporary staff, you won't always find people with exactly the right skills.

After discussion with your managers on what sort of personnel you *are* likely to have, you must revise the plan to take account of these factors:

- ⏱ *Familiarisation*. Every new member of the team will need some time to understand the overall problem, his tasks, and constraints on those tasks (e.g. technical standards). You should show this in your plan as a separate task for each person, before any productive work for that person.

- ⏱ *Personal productivity*. You may know that a particular individual is less (or more!) productive than the average you've used for your estimates. You can re-estimate that individual's tasks to take account of this, which may mean starting earlier or finishing later than your initial plan.

- ⏱ *New technology, standards etc*. Some aspects of the development environment may be new to one or more of the developers. Don't underestimate how long it will take them to get up to speed, particularly if there's a "paradigm shift" involved, like working with a fourth generation language or graphical user interface for the first time.

  There are a number of things you must do to cater for this. The most important is training: plan to have your people properly trained (if at all possible), *before* they are expected to contribute anything to the project. Secondly, allow an extra period of time while they come to terms with the new technology - they will inevitably work a little more slowly and make more mistakes while they are learning. Finally, choose low-criticality areas (or throw-away prototypes), rather than more important components, for the first experiments.

How Can I Present My Plan?

There are two prime requirements for the presentation of your plan: *clarity* and *maintainability*. It has to be understood by a large number of people. You have to be able to update it, easily. You can present your plan in tabular form (like on page 76), but it may be better to communicate the key information graphically.

The Gantt chart is the most common way of showing the tasks and milestones with their projected dates. This simply represents time along the X-axis and tasks as bars. The following is derived from the previous example using the project management package Microsoft Project:

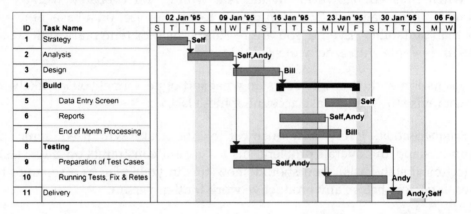

An alternative representation which is very useful for tracking dependencies and the critical path is known as the PERT chart. This shows the tasks as boxes, and the dependencies as links. The critical path can then be picked out (e.g. in bold, as below):

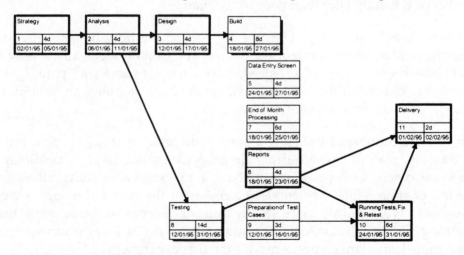

Your choice of representation will depend a little on the tools you have available. If you have access to project management software like Microsoft Project then you have a choice of formats and many of the calculations are automated, but beware! - this sort of tool may be "overkill" for a small project. If you only have a word-processor, then a tabular format is appropriate. If you have a spreadsheet, then a tabular format is easy, and with a little ingenuity you can also produce Gantt charts. If you only have pencil and paper then you *can* produce a plan, but updating it will be very hard work: even a word-processed version will be easier to work with.

Make the plan public. It's not some private agreement between you and your managers, but an honest declaration of what you believe you can achieve.

Invite comments on the plan, and be prepared to revise it if they seem reasonable. Most people will be much happier to work to the plan if they feel they've had a say in its creation, and they are working to estimates they have agreed. It's a good idea to call a meeting to discuss the estimates, which will then benefit from several viewpoints.

So whatever happened to the Grand Master Plan?

The plan is not cast in concrete but is a living thing. It *will* change. Be realistic in changing your plan to reflect changing circumstances and progress. Obviously, you will need to re-present your plan and get agreement to the changes. "Bullshit Planning" is all very well, but it will not help you explain to your users *why* you have not delivered to time, cost and quality.

You should expect pressure from your managers and users in respect of the overall timescales and costs, even if you believe your plan is realistic. Try to understand the business reasons for this pressure and see whether you can meet them. Maybe a phased delivery or an intermediate solution of some kind will address concerns on timescale. Postponing something may bring the costs back within budget. Remember that if cost and/or timescale are limited, then quality and functionality will also be limited. (See also "How Do I Resist Time and Budget Pressures?" on page 86.)

If you can, present any problem together with one possible solution: your managers will often "buy" that solution. Above all, be confident: if you are sure that your estimates are right, then don't bow to pressure to reduce them, or to compromise things like documentation and testing, instead of making proper adjustments to the scope and structure of the project.

How Do I Know I've Got The Estimates Correct?...

You don't! There isn't any crystal ball to consult. Instead, you need to pool experience to get good estimates - talk to your colleagues and managers and see what they think. Make sure at least two people estimate every task.

The proper way to size any job is to break it into a number of small tasks, each of which you feel you have a good chance of estimating, and then add the estimates together.

You will have to make some assumptions: for example that all your programmers are experienced, machines and people will be available to you, and you are working with a single technology. If these are not true then you need to add contingency. This should usually be at least 20%, and might be higher if you are unfamiliar with the technology or business.

If you keep good records of how large and complex each job is, and how much time it takes, then you can use this information to make much more accurate estimates in the future.

There are some "rules of thumb" you can apply to check that your estimates are sensible against other people's experience, but they are not a substitute for working out your own plan.

OK, so what sort of numbers should I get?

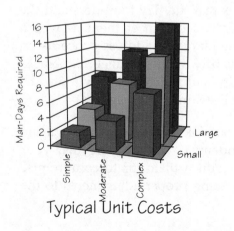

Typical Unit Costs

The classic way to check your estimates is to get a number for coding and unit testing, and then look at the ratio between that and other parts of the estimate:

The chart shows typical figures for "code and unit test" in man-days for an average programmer working in a high-level language. They assume roughly a 50-50 split between coding and ad-hoc testing on the one hand, and formal inspection and unit tests on the other.

Concentrate on getting the estimates for the complex and large programs right. It is these which will affect your delivery dates (if you get them wrong), not the small and easy screens and reports.

Keep it Small and Simple! (KISS!) If any estimate is larger than 5 days - then you have not defined the tasks in sufficient detail. Ten mandays is a long time if you have overrun on a project. If the estimate for any single program is this large, break it down into smaller elements for estimating and reporting purposes.

How do I estimate later testing?

You can estimate the number of likely test cases based on the number of requirements (allowing between 2 and 6 test cases per requirement). Then estimate how long it will take to produce them. Add an equal amount of effort (i.e. the estimated effort to produce the tests) for each execution of the tests.

Don't plan your testing effort on the assumption that no errors will be found! You *will* find errors - if you don't then your testing might not be good enough. You will then have to fix these errors, and re-test at least once. Thus your total test effort should be at least three times the cost of preparing the tests.

Overall, the total allowance for testing and test-related activities in your plan should be around 50%. If it's much less than 40%, then you haven't properly planned your testing.

What is the overall split between different stages?

The following is a "crude but successful" guide to the division of effort in a complete software development:

20%	Definition, design and planning
15%	Coding
15%	Component test & early system test
20%	Full system test, user testing & operational trials
20%	Documentation, training and implementation support
10%	Overall project management

Look how the "coding and component test" element is a small fraction (perhaps less than 20%) of the life-cycle total. Note also that this doesn't include the maintenance of the system - the overall life-cycle cost of a system may be even greater!

Isn't There a Better Way to Estimate Things?

There are some problems with this estimating and planning method. It involves a lot of hard work. You have to break the project down into relatively small tasks (which won't be fully identified until the project is part way through), and then get estimates for each task, from at least two people in each case. Ultimately, the total estimate is only as good as the individual estimates, and you don't really know the cost of building and testing the software until you're well into the Design stage.

These problems have led some people to look for an easier and more reliable way of estimating software development. However, it appears that most of them are no easier or more accurate, and may, in fact, involve extra work or inaccuracy.

The difficulty is there are so many variables in software development that no one job is exactly like another. Factors like the development language and environment, detailed requirements and programmer productivity vary enormously. Two programmers with supposedly similar skills can have productivity ratios of up to 10:1. Then you have to consider managerial factors like the stability of the requirements. Two supposedly similar systems (e.g. two "accounts payable" ledger systems) can easily differ in total cost by a factor of 100:1.

One type of estimating method starts by getting effort values for the "code and unit test" portion and taking these as a fixed proportion of the life-cycle. This is essentially the approach used in the previous section as a check on your estimates: it may be valid as a rough check, but not as a primary method for getting the estimates in the first place. There are two major problems: the size and shape of the build stage can't be known until you're well into design, and two projects with similar coding stages might have completely different problems in Analysis or Delivery.

A related approach (used by most of the named, "formal" estimating methods) is to try to measure (or estimate) one quantitative aspect of the project and scale costs and timescales from there. Typically, the basic value is a "line of code" (LOC).

But what is a LOC? Obviously not all lines of code are equal, and, more importantly, the number of lines of code vary dramatically between languages. Systems written in some fourth-generation languages (4GLs), or with the use of large libraries or a complex API (application programming interface) like most Windows software, have many lines of code which are not created by the project team and which you can't count. Do these count as lines of code? What about the declarative sections of many 4GLs (which you may not be able to view in the source code)? Even traditional 3GLs have related problems: do you count comment lines? White-space lines?

Again, there are two problems: the variation between environments is very wide, and you are trying to base your estimates on a number you won't know until you've written most of the programs! Many of the more complex estimating methods (for example COCOMO) are variants of this approach: be very wary if these are sold to you as magic ways of getting better estimates.

The alternative is to estimate based on something which is independent of design. The most obvious way is to try to count the functions which you have analysed, such as the entities and functions for a database, or objects, methods and properties for an object-oriented development. One quite successful formalised version of this is known as "Function Point Analysis". This is a good approach if you have a repeatable, structured method for analysis.

The remaining problem is that this (like the other methods) can show the relative size and difficulty of two projects, but not any absolute numbers. Such a method must be "calibrated" for the organisation, technology, team skills, problem domain, required quality and a large number of other factors. If you know the actual cost of one project, and can compare a second *similar* project using something like function points, then you can estimate the second project quite accurately. However, if your project is unlike anything you've done before, then your estimates won't be of great value.

Some books suggest that you can break your project down into areas based on your team's previous experience: some components of the system will be "off the shelf" and can be re-used exactly as they are, some you will have good, direct experience of, others you will have limited experience of, and a few (hopefully only a few) will be completely new to you. If you do this then at least you can base your estimates for some parts of the system on previous known costs, and you can do some risk management around the areas for which your estimate is likely to be less accurate.

So What Do You Conclude?

1.   Do lots of estimating, so you get better at it.

2.   Use something like function points to measure the size of your project in functional terms.

3.   Keep good records of the estimates and actual costs for each project. This is a sound investment for the future, because any estimating method is only as good as the historical data you calibrate it with - your best asset is a database of the characteristics and true costs of previous projects. If you have no such records, make a start *now*: if your project is split into phases and you keep good records now, you can get real payback estimating the later phases.

How Do I Resist Time and Budget Pressures?

Time pressure is *never* an acceptable excuse for not following the method and producing the required deliverables. The structured development process has grown up over a number of years as the only proven way of delivering quality information systems in a controlled fashion. You will usually take longer, overall, to deliver a system trying to cut corners than by following the method.

What do I do if I cannot meet the delivery timescales?

Sometimes you will simply not be able to deliver all the functionality to a delivery date which may be constrained by external events. In this case, the solution is simple: phased development. Divide your development up into phases, each of which will go through the full development process, but which you will deliver at different times.

Don't be pushed around - if you are sure of your estimates it is unlikely that any amount of force will magically make you deliver more quickly. *Don't* agree to omit important things like testing and documentation - without them the system may be functionally rich but will probably be useless to the users. However, *do* make sure your managers and sponsors understand if you are falling behind, and why.

What do I deliver first?

Take account of user priorities, but not to the detriment of the technical solution and sound project management. Within these constraints, and precedence constraints (e.g. data input functions will usually be necessary before output functions) follow the "Simplest First" rule: evaluate the cost, risk and benefit of each element, and provide the elements in descending order of value (calculated as *Benefit/(Cost*Risk)*).

What do I do if the budget is insufficient?

Deliver fewer functions, and ask for more money! It is *always* a mistake to try to deliver more functions by skimping on things like testing and documentation. This will invariably result in higher maintenance costs, and the life-cycle cost will far exceed the budget. Some things are scaleable (within limits), like the provision of user documentation, but as a general rule if the budget appears insufficient the only sensible option is to challenge the requirements and try to simplify or reduce them, or deliver in separately funded phases. Get the users to prioritise the functions, and then to sign off a plan which follows these priorities.

There is no inverse link between quality and productivity. If you consider another industry (car production, for example), then the most productive companies (e.g. Toyota) are also the ones producing high quality. It's the same in software. Keeping the quality high doesn't usually mean delivering later, and reducing the quality doesn't necessarily mean delivering earlier. Instead, it probably means more wasted time and lost deadlines at the end of the project caused by quality-related problems.

How Do I Handle Criticism of My Estimates?

Make sure your estimates are well structured, clearly presented and have been checked by both experienced colleagues and some who will be *doing* the work. Formal estimates are much harder to criticise than one man's "finger in the air".

If you can, refer to the costs of previous comparable projects. If you manage the project much better, or the requirements are much more stable, then your costs might be rather lower, but you can't assume those things (*yet!*). Otherwise, don't expect your costs to be much lower: things like different tools or technology might make a difference of a few percent, but it won't be much more than that. *Do* make a note of any special difficulties on your project that you already know about.

Remember, and explain, that testing or CASE tools, new methods etc. will only show a benefit if *used*, and if you allow for proper training and learning curves early on. They won't show any benefit (and might have a net negative effect) if they're introduced too quickly or seen as an imposition from above.

Think about the accuracy of your estimates, and quote all your numbers with an error range (e.g. "100 man-days ± 10"). Remember to add up the errors as well as the "best guess" numbers. Then try to show some relationship between the overall accuracy of your estimates and the contingency level.

How Should I Allow for Problems?

You need to allow a sensible "contingency fund" on your estimates. Different people have different rules for what is "sensible": in this book I've said 20%. If possible, this should bear some relationship to the accuracy of your estimates. *Don't* allow this to be cut to reduce the overall estimates - insist on cutting some functions instead.

Create a small budget for investigating and documenting changes to the requirements. If you make sure that changes are properly documented and the effort is "billed" against this fund, it will help to keep the changes separate and controlled, when the users realise they are using it up.

What is the "Testing Trap"?

Don't be tempted to treat documentation and (*even worse!*) testing as an optional extra that you can do when the development is "finished". This is a sure-fire recipe for disaster. For example, you could fall into the "testing trap". Our typical project plan looks rather like this:

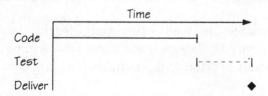

Yes, I know it should be 50% code and 50% testing, but do *you* actually *do* that? The next thing that happens is that coding takes a bit longer than expected (it *does* happen), but we still want to hit the same delivery date, don't we? So now our plan looks like this:

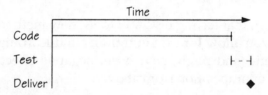

OK, you tell me. Is this system going to be properly tested? Not only have we reduced the amount of testing, but we know that there were problems building it, so there are probably more errors to find, not less. The *only* way to avoid this is to plan your testing (and documentation) as continuous (or periodic) activities that run alongside the build jobs:

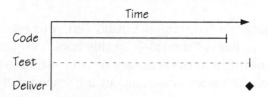

There are several ways you can do this. You can have part of your team constantly working on testing the work of the rest. You can get two programmers to "swap" and test each other's work after they've finished a pair of jobs, or you can alternate weeks of build and testing work for the whole team. It's your choice!

What Other Resources Do I Need?

People aren't the only resources you need to estimate and plan for. If you don't have desks or computers for them, your expensive human resources aren't going to be much good! There are other resources you will need through the project. Make sure you identify your requirements clearly and early enough that there is a reasonable chance for them to be met. If there is likely to be any shortcoming in the provision, you need to put a contingency plan into place.

Although the non-human resources are often quite inexpensive compared with the human ones, this doesn't mean they will be easy to arrange. Things like space and computer equipment may be controlled by different managers through different budgets, and it'll be up to you to make a case for them, allowing adequate lead-time.

Remember that the staffing of your project will start at a low level, reach a peak during the build stage, and then drop off again to a lower level. (See "How Do I Plan the Staffing of the Project?" on page 78 and the example on page 76.) You need to anticipate the rise in staffing, but it's not a bad idea to allow a bit of leeway before you promise to give things (or people) back!

As a very rough guide, you'll need about 100 square feet ($10m^2$) of space for each member of the team, plus space for machines, books, documents etc. You'll need room for meetings and where people can work together without disturbing others - you may be able to share this with other projects. Every developer will need a desk, a terminal or PC, and accounts for the development environment, the applications, email and so on. Don't try to economise by making too many developers share these things - it's always a false economy which will result in them failing (or refusing) to use the right tools and procedures. Similarly, make sure that developers are trained, properly and early, in the tools, standards and procedures they will use.

Think about any specialist equipment and software needs. As well as your development environment, you'll need word-processors and spreadsheets. You may need test and CASE tools, but they're not essential unless they're required by the methods and standards you follow. You may have to share some specialist tools.

Create a plan describing all these things, saying *what* you'll need, *why* and *when*. Then *communicate* this to those responsible for the other resources, and chase hard to make sure things happen when they should.

   Peopleware should help you to marshal your arguments on the need for proper equipment and space for software developers.

What Do I Do If I'm Not Meeting My Plan?

Multiple choice: your regular progress checks suggest to you that a task on the critical path is likely to exceed its budget and timescale by about 50%. Do you:

a.   Run around the office shouting "Oh my God, we're all going to die!".

b.   Have a quiet chat with the group responsible for the task and find out what the problem is. There are three likely cases:

   ♠ There is a difficult technical problem. The best solutions to this are a brainstorming session, or temporarily moving your best problem-solver onto the team with the problem. You will need to re-plan the tasks he or she was working on.

   ♠ There is nothing intrinsically difficult about the task, but the individual(s) working on it are not sufficiently skilled to make good progress. The short-term fix is probably to have someone more skilled work alongside them or take over part of the task. If you do decide to swap tasks between people, then make sure you re-plan allowing for the lower skill level which will now be on a different task, and for familiarisation time for all concerned.

   ♠ The team are making reasonable progress, but the task is just much larger than expected. You may be able to make up some of the lost time by switching other resources onto the task or working overtime, but there are limits to this: no-one ever recouped more than about 20-30% this way. If you need more people or time you'll have to ask your managers for more budget, and revise your plan to take account of the slippage.

c.   Go down to the pub on your own and get very drunk.

d.   Hold a meeting of the team at the pub to discuss the nature of the problem and possible solutions (see option b).

e.   Stop your reporting and checking - it's obviously not working.

f.   Increase the frequency of reporting and checking while the problem remains.

g.   Cancel all holidays and tell everyone to work an extra 5 hours a week.

h.   Immediately move your best resources onto the task with the problem, abandoning whatever they are working on.

i.   Revise your plan, moving resources around if necessary. Note that if you move resources from other tasks onto this one, the tasks they were working on may now, because of the lower staffing, be on the critical path.

j.   Review your plan to see whether the same problem is likely to occur on any other tasks which you haven't yet started.

k.   Write a memo to your managers and the key user saying what you've found, what you've done about it and the net effect you think it may have.

l.   Write a memo to your managers and the key user resigning your post.

m.   None of the above (and hope the problem will go away).

Score 5 points (*very good*) if your answer was some combination of b, d, f, i, j and k. Score 0 points (*depressingly average*) if you included any of a, c, e, g, h, l or m.

Obviously, the earlier you know, the better. Unless you have good, regular reporting against a plan you won't find the problem until it's too late (and some combination of a, c, e, g, h or l are your only way out!).

Overtime is a very limited solution to anything. If you are making good progress on a job which is just bigger than expected you might get an extra 10% effort through overtime. You're unlikely to get any more than this without either reducing the quality and productivity of the work, or damaging other areas of the work, and you can't keep it up forever.

Unless you've just got the wrong man on a job (and the right man or woman can be moved onto it) you're not going to get more than about a 10-20% improvement by adding manpower to a task. Remember Brooks' Law.

> Adding manpower to a late software project makes it later.
> Frederick P Brooks

What this means is that you have to recoup any slippage over a number of tasks, not just one. You *must* revise your plan, both to take account of the new resources and known slippage, and to look for any other tasks which may have the same problem.

A problem shared is someone else's problem too! Don't be afraid to discuss things *promptly* with your team and managers. They may see a solution you may be missing, or at least they'll be better prepared for adjustments to the budget or timescale if these have to be made.

So How Should I Create My Plan?

1. You must have a plan. The plan is a tool for *your* use: a road-map through the various tasks, and a way of finding out whether you are on target or not.

2. Make sure your plan includes all the tasks in the project.

3. Don't plan on the basis that everything will go right: it won't!

4. Make your estimates realistic. Get them checked by senior colleagues and those who will actually do the work. Plan for non-project activities in your schedules.

5. There is no guaranteed way of getting estimates right. There are some good rules of thumb, but your best tool is a database of historical information about the actual costs of other projects.

6. A good plan should answer the six key questions *what? why? when? where? how?* and *who?* for every task. Your plan should clearly show timescales, deadlines and deliverables.

7. Review your resources and any constraints, then match the resources to the tasks and turn your estimated task breakdown into a full schedule of work.

8. Don't be bullied into accepting a plan you cannot meet. Know the arguments against unrealistic time and budget pressures.

9. There are various options for maintaining and presenting your plan. The key requirements, whatever your choice, are *clarity* and *maintainability*.

10. Make the plan public. Use it as a mechanism to communicate with your team, managers and users. Invite comments and make sure you get agreement to it.

11. The plan is a living thing. Keep it up-to-date.

12. If you detect slippage against the plan, *don't panic!*. Think carefully about the nature of the problem(s), and revise your plan to include a solution.

📖 The best discussions of estimating methods (in a lot more detail than here) are in *Controlling Software Projects* and *Software Project Management*. The former book is very comprehensive and contains some good advice on function-based estimating, although it is really aimed at a metrics specialist.

The Strategy

The Strategy stage (also called by many other names, including "Problem Definition" and "Feasibility Study") is where you decide what the objectives of your project are, and whether they are feasible and justified.

The main aim is to find out what business problems you are expected to solve, and investigate the options for their solution. You may have to consider whether the solutions are justified in terms of their benefit to the business, and whether they fit within the budget. The main outcome will be a report describing the problems and possible solutions, with a recommendation on what your users and managers should do.

During this stage, you'll need to make the first stab at a project plan, and create a Quality Plan outlining how the project is to be run, what standards and procedures you are going to use, and who has what responsibilities. You'll need to assess what quality of system is required, and match the possible solutions to this requirement.

In order to make a good start, you'll also need to set up the filing and reporting structures for the project, and start using them as you mean to go on!

What is the Role of A Strategy?

The role of any Strategy is five-fold:

1.   Define *what* you are going to do, and *when*.

2.   Define *what* you are *not* going to do.

3.   Define what other people have to do (*who*)

4.   *Prove* that all this is justified and funded (*why* and *how*).

5.   *Prove* that all this is feasible (*how* and *where*).

You might think number 1 is the most important, but you'd be wrong! You've got all of the Analysis stage to assess *what* the user wants, and all of the Design stage to define *How* to provide it. However, if you don't start very early to manage the user's expectations, then the *what* will grow out of control, and you may not have enough freedom on the *how*, either. So it's absolutely vital to make sure the scope of any development, and its boundaries, are well defined. This is number 2.

It's also essential that you are sure you are going to get the support, information, funding and effort you need, particularly from the users (item 3). If you are not, it's better to discover this now than get trapped later in the project when the costs and risks of failure are climbing rapidly.

The Strategy Report must be able to prove that this is all OK. Things like signed Declarations of Objectives and approved Quality Plans go a long way to building your confidence, and everyone else's, that you are likely to succeed.

You may need to *prove* that it's all justified (item 4). Think carefully about the total cost of the exercise: consider the costs of development or procurement, the costs of the hardware and infrastructure it will run on, and the costs that the users and support teams will incur introducing the system. Don't forget the "hidden" costs such as data loading, training and documentation.

Balanced against this must be the benefit to the business of the automated solution. The users should be able to show how this will be measured and demonstrate the benefit, but you must understand the business case. Be realistic: if the new system will cost £100 000 ($150 000), and might save the cost of two clerical members of staff, then the pay-back period is at least three years. Such a system probably isn't justified.

Be prepared to *Challenge The Requirements*, and *Keep It Simple, Stupid!* Maybe there is a business case for a simple, cheap system, but not for a complicated one. If you need a guard dog, specify and buy something like on the left. Don't try to specify and build something like on the right: if you do it'll cost far too much, probably won't work and will cause problems you didn't have before! (See *Jurassic Park* for details!)

The other thing a Strategy must do is to prove there is at least one feasible way of delivering the required functions, and choose positively between a choice of solutions (item 5). *Don't leap at the first technical solution that comes to mind - do the analysis first! Don't* assume that it has to be a custom development or a major procurement. Spend time thinking about whether there is a simpler solution - possibly not involving computers at all! If you can't think of two ways to solve the problem, you're either not looking hard enough, or you (or the users) are trapped into prescribing the *how* rather than understanding the *what*. This is another recipe for disaster!

Use the Strategy stage of a development to establish and test the roles and responsibilities of the various parties to the development. The users should define what they want, and the business benefits it will deliver. You should challenge these requirements, and see if you can deliver comparable benefits in a simpler way. You should establish possible solutions and their costs, and propose a preferred solution. Remember, *you* are the technical specialist, *not* the users.

You must document the way in which you are going to proceed early enough that if there is any problem, the project can be stopped or changed before too much money is spent. For this reason, the Strategy documents must be produced and approved *before* any work is done. Just like moving out into heavy traffic, *wait if you are not sure it's safe to proceed*. It's much better to halt or delay a project early on and get the assurances everyone needs, rather than to hurry through, avoiding the issues - if you do this you will get badly burnt later on.

If the users don't know what they want, analyse the way they plan to do business, *not* the tools they think they might like. Then look for areas of business where there is a clear benefit from automation. If you can't find any, the users don't need a computer system.

How Do I Make a Business Case?

You must justify the development and/or introduction of a computer system in one or more of the following ways:

☺   The system is forced on the organisation for some external reason (e.g. legal requirements or technical necessity). In this case, the aim must be to find some secondary benefit from the system, or keep its costs to an absolute minimum.

☺   The system can be sold at a net profit over its development costs. In this case, you will have to show the size of the market, your likely share of it and the price which the system will sustain (probably by comparison with competitive products). Offset against this must be the costs of development, marketing, distribution and support.

☺   The system will reduce the operating costs of the organisation by a larger amount than its own costs. The potential benefit in this case is usually a reduction or redeployment of manpower currently doing the tasks the computer will assist or automate. As well as the costs of the computer system itself, you need to take into account the costs of restructuring the workforce (including things like the costs of redundancies or retraining). The costs of any change to an organisation's structure can be quite high.

☺   The system will boost the sales of the organisation, typically by improving the range or quality of the goods and services offered by the organisation. The increase in sales will exceed the system's costs. In some cases, this may be forced on the users if the competition have already gained similar benefits.

☺   The system will provide a new capability whose value exceeds the system's cost. The "value" relates either to the cost of *not* doing the new function, or to the cost of doing it by the cheapest alternative means (probably a manual one), whichever is the *lower*.

You need to decide which of these categories apply, and develop a clear estimate of the total costs and benefits of the system over the years from its inception. The users should help you to evaluate the benefit and any non-development costs. You may need to include things like the costs of financing the development, or the opportunity cost of that money being used elsewhere. The *payback period* is the period after the first money is spent when the costs exceed the benefits. At the end of this period the benefits should start to exceed costs and there will be a net benefit from the system. The following cashflow shows how these figures might look for one system:

	1994	1995	1996	1997	1998
Balance Carried Forward		(£25 000)	(£65 000)	(£32 000)	£6 000
Development Costs	(£20 000)	(£30 000)			
Software Maintenance		(£5 000)	(£10 000)	(£10 000)	(£10 000)
Hardware	(£5 000)	(£10 000)			
Staff Retraining/Restructuring		(£20 000)	(£2 000)	(£2 000)	(£2 000)
Reduction in Production Costs		£25 000	£30 000	£30 000	£30 000
Increased Sales from Quality Improvements			£15 000	£20 000	£25 000
Net Benefit (Cost)	(£25 000)	(£65 000)	(£32 000)	£6 000	£49 000

The payback period of this system is almost four years. The eventual benefits may be quite high, but the business has to fund a capital expenditure of £65 000 for four years to pay for them, and the business decision may be that the costs (especially if there is any risk they may be underestimated) are too high.

There will inevitably be a trade-off between functionality, quality and cost. You may have to repeat the cost/benefit assessment for several different options:

Option	Total Cost	Total Benefit after 4 Years	Net benefit after 4 Years	Payback Period
The "Mini"	£5 000	£10 000	£5 000	2 years
The "Escort"	£30 000	£50 000	£20 000	4 years
The "Rolls-Royce"	£100 000	£90 000	-£10 000	never?

Which would you go for? The "Mini" doesn't really deliver much benefit, and it may be a false economy (if, for example, it doesn't provide a good basis for future expansion). However, if resources are limited it might be a good start. The "Escort" has a respectable benefit, but a longer pay-back period. This is probably the best bet, but you need to be really sure about the costs and benefits.

On these figures, the "Rolls-Royce" can't be justified - it may never pay for itself. If, however, the competition has a "Rolls-Royce" and you need this level of functionality to stay in business, then the company may make a business decision to go ahead. If this happens, you must make sure everyone is fully aware of the real costs of doing so. Make sure the decision is taken at a senior enough level, and then find the most cost effective way of providing that system.

Be very careful to make your business case realistic. People are notoriously optimistic about expected benefits, and it's easy to exceed software cost estimates. But there are no prizes for a well-managed project which actually costs the company money.

How Do I Know What Quality is Required?

All solutions are not equal. Part of the equation in deciding which problems to solve and how to solve them is the *quality* required from the solution. How "good" should your system be? The answer isn't necessarily "excellent" if that's going to cost a fortune and isn't justified. "Good enough" is the right answer, but how good is "good enough"?

The quality of a software system is a combination of a number of factors, including:

Q   *Adaptability.* Can system functions be created or modified easily?
Q   *Completeness.* Are all the documented functions delivered and consistent?
Q   *Data Quality.* How accurate & complete is the data stored in the system?
Q   *Efficiency.* What machine resources does it use? Does it work quickly enough?
Q   *Friendliness.* How easy is the system to use? Is it ergonomically sound?
Q   *Maintainability.* Can the current functions of the software be maintained?
Q   *Portability.* Can the system be migrated to other environments if necessary?
Q   *Reliability.* How often does the system fail to perform its functions?
Q   *Resilience.* How does the system respond to user errors or external problems?
Q   *Security.* Is the system protected against unauthorised access and corruption?
Q   *Testability.* How easily can the system be tested?
Q   *Timeliness.* Will the software be available, properly implemented, when needed?

What you have to do is to define clear, preferably *measurable* requirements for each of these factors. These requirements must be *testable*: you must be able to *prove* that you have met them. There are a number of questions you can ask which will help you decide what the quality requirements should be:

?   *Who will use the software?* The number, variety and skill level of users is critical in determining system quality. A system destined for a large number of users, with varying (and sometimes quite low) computer skills must be reliable and easy to use. You may decide to simplify the system at the cost of "power" features which would only be used by a small percentage of users. Documentation, training and support will have to be comprehensive and of a high quality.

If, on the other hand, the system is going to be used by two or three users who will become very familiar with it, then ease of use features may be superfluous, and you may even decide that they can tolerate lower reliability.

?   *What is the Cost of Failure?* What will happen if the system fails to perform its functions. The answer will be somewhere on a scale between "potential loss of life" and "the users will be a bit frustrated, but the organisation can still function quite well". Factors like reliability and maintainability will have to be very high in the former case, but can be lower in the latter case.

? *How good is the users' control? How good will the data be?* If the system will be used in an environment where its use isn't controlled, and the quality of the data being input will be poor, you have to make a decision whether aspects like security and data integrity are actually important. If so, the system must try to impose some measure of control. If not, then the requirements on the system may be quite lax.

? *Are there time-critical operations? What is the relative cost of software and hardware?* If there are few requirements on performance, or if hardware is relatively cheap, then you don't need to worry much about efficiency. Otherwise, you need to specify comprehensive, *quantitative* requirements for performance.

? *How stable are the requirements?* If the business is changing, or the requirements aren't very certain, then adaptability is important. As well as making your system adaptable, you should employ other techniques to try and better manage the requirements (see the rest of this chapter).

? *What is more important, the functions or the delivery date?* If the latter, then you may need to limit or phase the requirements in order to deliver a sufficiently high-quality system by the deadline.

Remember that there is no inverse link between the number of errors in software, and productivity. You should *always* be aiming to deliver software with the minimum possible number of *errors*, since that will probably be cheapest over the lifetime of the system. What we are discussing here are the various non-functional requirements, not whether lots of bugs are acceptable or not.

You will express most of these quality requirements either in the requirement specification for the system, or as constraints in the project plan. The Quality Plan is mainly a mechanism for documenting the structure of the project, the methods and standards which you will use, and the roles and responsibilities of the various people involved (see page 102). However, the required quality of the system will help to determine what project structure and standards are appropriate, so you need to get a good grasp of the required quality before you finalise the Quality Plan.

What Else Do We Need to Decide?

The nature and structure of the project will depend on a number of important decisions on matters such as the methods you are going to use, the way you will test the software, and the approach to user documentation. For each main option in your Strategy Report, you need to think (and document) what your approach will be. Then, as you get nearer to a decision on the preferred option, these will become part of the Quality Plan (or the first draft of the Test and Documentation Strategies).

What Analysis and Design Techniques Are We Going to Employ?

You will need to choose an appropriate set of techniques for analysis and design, depending on the likely approach to the project. For example, if you are thinking of buying in a package solution from outside, then there may not be too much point in doing detailed dataflow diagrams in the Analysis stage (although you may want something with which to check the fit of the different packages). On the other hand, if your application is going to be a large custom-made database, then you *must* do some form of data structure analysis, such as entity-relationship modelling.

You need to think about the three "degrees of freedom" of a system:

➜ the functions that the system provides to the user,

↑ the static structure of the data retained in the system,

↗ the life-cycle of data, and the dynamic changes to it.

If one or more of these aspects is constrained by the proposed solution (e.g. the static data structure of a package), or is trivial (e.g. the dynamic behaviour of a database used mainly for queries), then you may not need to model that aspect. Otherwise, you need to choose an Analysis technique and a Design technique which will model each aspect. Although your choice may be constrained by your methods and tools, you should still make the best choice you can.

See "Which Techniques Should I Use?" on page 124 for more details.

What Documentation Are We Going to Produce?

The requirements for user and technical documentation, training and support will vary depending on several factors including the number and skills of the users and the different jobs they perform, whether or not you are basing your project on a package or existing system, and the amount of change to any such system. Decide what documentation must be produced for your system, when, and by whom; and the responsibilities for training and support. If these can be agreed, at least in principle, during the Strategy stage then you can formalise the responsibilities through the Quality Plan, and allow properly for the tasks and effort required (in the Project Plan).

See "What About User Documentation?" on page 172 for more details.

What Level of Testing is Required?

The amount, nature and timing of software testing will depend on a number of factors, including:

&ᴄ the required quality of the system,

&ᴄ whether it's a bespoke (custom) development, or a package (whose internals you probably can't test),

&ᴄ whether the development will be in-house or external (in which case you won't be able to do much early testing),

&ᴄ what technology is being employed (some are easier to test than others),

&ᴄ the availability of appropriate test experts, tools and standards.

The Test Strategy will document the expected structure (method) of testing, which test techniques you will use, and the interaction with other developers and projects with which your system interfaces. The principles should be agreed during the Strategy stage and documented in the Quality Plan.

See "How Do I Do Good Testing?" on page 170 for more details.

What is a Quality Plan?

The Quality Plan is the document in which you formally define the form of the project: the structure of the project, the methods and standards you will use, and who has what responsibilities. It is important to get a Quality Plan agreed at an early stage of the project, as otherwise you may find that you have been building a system for the wrong person, or to unacceptable standards.

Who makes the decisions? This is probably the single most important question to get a definitive, documented answer to. You may find that you have considerable freedom over how the project is run, and you are talking to one or two users who are free to decide the requirements, budget and timescales. However, it's much more likely that your managers will impose certain limits on your decision-making ability, and the users' managers will do the same. You may have to get all major documents signed off by these more senior people, or by a committee representing several interest groups.

Who Makes
the Decisions?

Whatever the situation is, you need to carefully document it (defining the limits of responsibility if possible), and get it signed off by your own managers, and the senior user managers. This is especially important if they are happy to devolve some decision making power to you and your direct contacts. Take the agreed situation into account both in defining procedures (e.g. for document approval) and in creating your plans. Be realistic. For example, there's no point in having to have a committee of 10 people to sign everything off, and then allowing only one day per document (in elapsed time) for the sign-off process. You just won't get people organised that quickly.

Who are you building the system for? This is not necessarily the same as the previous point! Quite often, you will be instructed to build a system for a variety of users or user groups. You need to make sure that requirements, prototypes, tests and so forth involve representatives of all these groups.

Who will do what? What are the different roles in the project team and the user group? What tasks will these people do? What will they *not* do?

What will be the project structure? What decisions have you made about the structure of the project? Will you follow a defined structured method, or are you going to do something different? What are the criteria for starting and ending each stage of the work?

What standards and QA procedures will you follow? Obviously, this depends a bit on your decisions about project structure. You need to document all the key procedures (like change control, document approval etc.), and what technical standards will apply to different parts of the work.

What deliverables are you going to produce? The output of each part of the work will be a defined deliverable. This deliverable should have a defined content, and be subject to a defined process of review or testing so that it can be formally approved.

How are you going to do configuration management? How will the different documents and software components which make up the project be identified? How will you mark different versions? What tools or techniques will you use for controlling the changes between versions? Where will software and documents be stored? How will items be approved for inclusion in a software release?

The Quality Plan should include details of the QA organisation, procedures for procurement and any subcontract work, and how you will plan, monitor and report progress. In most cases, you'll have separate documents describing the structure of testing, and the approach you're going to take to user documentation and training. However, on a small project you might also include these within the Quality Plan.

Obviously, this could be an enormous amount of writing (and reading!). However, you will probably be following a method and standards which are defined in detail either in a book, or in your organisation's Quality Manual and related documents. In this case, what you can quite reasonably do is refer to the appropriate document, and then just document the *differences* (things which you are going to do differently, or not at all) and *specific details* (i.e. names, dates etc.) which apply to your own project.

Don't imagine that this lets you quote standards which are inappropriate (or which you have no intention of following) and then just ignore them. If your project fails, or is audited for any reason, the first thing that will be checked is whether you have followed the procedures in your Quality Plan. It is your duty to choose, document and get agreement to sensible procedures and standards for your project.

The fundamental principles of Quality standards (such as the international standard ISO 9000 and its variants) are:

✓   Say what you are going to do
✓   Do what you said
✓   Document, so you can *prove* you did it

The Quality Plan sets up the framework so you can do this.

What Goes Into the Strategy Report?

The contents of the Strategy Report should include the following:

Q The scope and objectives of the document. List areas *not* covered in the document. Assess how much more work you must do before a go-ahead decision can be made.

Q An account of the purpose of the proposed system, and any special benefits that may accrue from its introduction, or particular problems to be solved.

Q The functional boundaries (scope) of the system. Detail any areas of function which have been identified but which you are specifically *not* going to analyse or develop. It may be appropriate to include at this point a brief account of external interfaces.

Q Any simplifying assumptions, budgetary or time constraints, externally-imposed limits on the choice of solution etc.

Q Unresolved issues. Any issues likely to affect the completeness of the problem definition or the choice of solution which you have been unable to resolve.

Q Terminology and abbreviations.

Q Problem definition. This might form the basis of the Statement of Requirements in the Analysis stage. It should concentrate on an analysis of the current business and any particular changes required to the way the business operates:

- Problems to be solved.

- Critical success factors.

- Functional requirements (functions to be provided, stated in business terms).

- Data structures (static & dynamic), in enough detail to support the functional requirements. You should not view the models created as a constraint on possible solutions.

- User profile.

- Technical & quality requirements.

Q   List of potential solutions. These should include "do nothing" and any manual solutions to the problems.

Q   Comparison of potential solutions. This should compare each of the possible solutions, describing for each:

- An outline description of the potential solution, both functional and technical, but concentrating on particular strengths or weaknesses (compared with your known requirements).

- Cost/benefit analysis.

- Risk analysis.

- Quality requirements and constraints (for example, you might be aware of a package solution, but this won't meet the adaptability requirements).

- Test strategy (how much testing is required compared with other options).

- Documentation strategy (again, sufficient to compare solutions and make sure the total costs are understood).

Q   Recommendations and next steps. This should select one of the possible approaches as the recommendation, explaining in particular why you have rejected cheaper or simpler approaches. (Of course, it might also conclude that none of the solutions are adequate). It should then provide a bit more detail on:

- Summary of problem, proposed solution and status.

- Development approach.

- Required approval / funding / resources.

- Next steps (e.g. work required before formal approval), or the plan for the next stage.

- Concerns about the proposals. In particular, any major risks which require further investigation or immediate action.

Remember, you don't get paid by weight! The important thing is to marshal the *key* requirements and characteristics of each solution, plus a good analysis of the costs, benefits and risks. If you happen to uncover a wealth of analytical detail, or there are clear pointers towards the likely design, then document these separately.

How Do I Control Communications with People?

Start as you mean to go on, and be formal! Insist on good habits from the beginning. If you can get your team and users used to the idea that communications must be formalised, then they will follow your lead automatically. If, on the other hand, you attempt to introduce better practices part of the way through a project, when there are already severe problems, you are unlikely to succeed.

The main principle is that every communication external to the team (with your managers, users or vendors) must be either written, or confirmed in writing. At first, this may seem excessive and bureaucratic, but you'll be amazed how quickly it seems natural. On the other hand, it only takes one "lost" or mis-understood telephone conversation with a user to cause considerable disruption to your careful plan! In the same way, it's important to minute meetings, or at least their conclusions. Writing can't be your only form of communication, but it must be the formal way.

Keep the formal lines of communication between your team and the "outside world" to a minimum. Ideally, all communications with a vendor should be between yourself and the vendor's project manager. The bulk of communication with the users should be between yourself and a small number of key users. This helps to reduce the possibility of conflicting messages, or of messages not reaching their intended target.

However, this does mean that when you issue or receive a communication, you must make sure that you copy it to everyone who needs to know. Although at times this may seem like an unnecessary load on people, it will reduce the number of mistakes because of mis-information. In any case, keeping people informed will help to create the open, informative environment which is vital if your aim is good quality. If you have electronic mail you can set up project-wide automatic distribution lists.

Keep a file of all formal communications - the Project File. You should store any communication on which you need to take action (e.g. a change request) in the file and also on a separate log sheet (or database) which you can check to see that the appropriate actions have been taken.

You may be lucky enough to have some administrative or tool support for all of this. If so, then *use* it! However, even if you don't, you must make sure that you keep communications under control.

(See also "How do I know if I'm communicating properly?" on page 32.)

What Do I Deliver?

The following is a typical set of deliverables from a Strategy stage:

- *Declaration of Objectives*. This short document should ideally be produced by the decision-makers on the users' side. If not, it *must* be signed off by them. It must set out the overall business and organisational objectives for the project, and any major limitations of scope or constraints they wish to impose. This will normally only be re-issued if there's a major change of scope for the system.

- *Quality Plan*. This sets out the roles and responsibilities for the project, the overall project structure, and the methods, standards and procedures which you will adopt. This will be maintained throughout the life of the project. (See page 102 for details.)

- *Strategy Report*. This describes the problems which the project must solve, and then analyses the options for the solution. On the basis of this analysis, you can make a set of recommendations, for management approval. This document won't normally be maintained, but parts of it may evolve into the Analysis Report. (See page 104 for details.)

- *Project Plan*. This should present an outline plan for the chosen solution, in enough detail to support the costs and timescales in the Strategy Report, and in detail for the Analysis stage. It will be maintained throughout the life of the project, and used as the basis for progress monitoring and reporting.

- *Models*. If a custom development is likely, then you will probably produce high-level versions of the various functional and data models, which will be enhanced through the Analysis stage. These may form part of the Strategy Report.

- *Project File*. You need to set up the project filing system for documentation and correspondence. If you are going to control correspondence through some form of control system (whether automated or manual), then the Strategy stage is a good time to get this started. You will certainly need a system for change requests and related documentation. (See page 106 for details.)

- *Software Project Management* contains useful check-lists for the contents of a Quality Plan in the form of a *Software Quality Assurance Plan* and *Software Configuration Management Plan*.

Analysis

In Analysis you define the requirements for the system you will buy or build. It consists of the following main tasks:

1. Identify the users' goals, and describe the business processes that the system will support.

2. Analyse, describe and structure the data the users will process.

3. Find out where data will come from, and go to.

4. Describe what use will be made of the data (the reporting functions).

"I'll go and find out what they need, and the rest of you start coding!"

5. Plan how to test that the functions have been delivered.

Note that we haven't made any mention of the system structure which will support the functions. This is not an Analysis issue. You must concentrate on the business processes which any system must support, not specific implementations of these processes, whether existing or planned.

This is equally true when you are defining enhancements to an existing system: base the Analysis on understanding the business functions and data currently supported and the changes required to that structure. Only then can you be sure that the changes to the system design will have the right result for the business.

I assume you will be doing at least part of the analysis work. If not, then make sure your architect or analyst reads this, and make sure you fully understand the requirements and models he or she produces.

What Do They Need?

The main aim of Analysis is to take the scope and high-level description of the users' requirements, and turn it into a detailed set of requirements from which you can either procure, or design and build the system.

You have to do this before you start the Design, otherwise you don't know what you are designing. There's often a great temptation, once you've got the go-ahead to the Strategy, to leap into the design and build and "get something done", but this almost always results in a system which does not match the users' actual needs. If you have to start doing major surgery to accommodate user requirements which you didn't bother to analyse, then no matter how good your design and code, they will end up confused, undocumented and unreliable.

For this reason, you need to keep the analysis in "business terms": in terms of the real-world objects and business operations which the system will have to support. If you start to phrase the "requirements" in terms of what you think the solution will be, there are dangers:

- You may understand the more design-related terminology, but your users won't. As a result, they won't be able or inclined to spot errors or contribute to the analysis.

- You will automatically think in terms of one design, when there may be a number of options to consider. Your first thoughts on design may not suit the total set of requirements, when you understand the full picture.

I know it's difficult to do this if your background is in design or programming, but it's absolutely essential!

The other thing to watch out for is allowing the scope of the system to grow out of control. It's awfully easy when you're writing down detailed requirements to add things you hadn't previously thought of. You must be rigorous: if a requirement is outside the system's scope as defined in the Strategy Report, then treat it as a change request, and get it properly approved before you add it in.

These warnings also apply when you are defining enhancements to an existing system: you must base the Analysis stage on understanding the business functions and data currently supported and the changes required to that structure. Only then can you be sure that the changes will have the right result for the business.

How Can I Check the Requirements?

Use models to capture and communicate the business processes, data, structure and functions. Models have a number of advantages over bulk text: they are more compact and less ambiguous. They should be easier to update, and there are techniques which you can apply to check that the models are self-consistent (see "Which Techniques Should I Use?" on page 124). Remember: a picture is worth a thousand words.

If you are using use cases, every aspect of the model should tie in to at least one user goal. If not, then you may be specifying things which are not required.

For each data item, ask yourself "Where and when is this data created?". If you don't know, then there are major functions you haven't analysed.

For each requirement to store data, ask yourself "Why is this data needed?". There is no point whatsoever in capturing data unless you have a clear idea of how, when and why it is going to be used. This means that you have to understand the *output* functions in comparable detail to the *input* functions. Make sure you understand which data and uses are mandatory, and which merely desirable.

Thinking about testing is a key Analysis activity. For each requirement, ask yourself "How can I test this?". If you can't think of a simple, unambiguous test to check whether a requirement is satisfied, you haven't yet defined that requirement well enough. If you write down these test cases at the same time as the requirements, then you have the starting point for an excellent set of system tests.

If you have to interface with other systems, check that you understand the business processes which require the transfer of data or control between the systems. If you understand the reasons, then the details will be much easier to understand.

Make the users think about their procedures for using the system. Since these procedures need to work even if the system is not available, many of them will be quite independent of the detailed structure of the system. Make sure you understand the current thinking on the user organisation and procedures, and highlight any inconsistencies with your analysis. This is particularly important if the user organisation or business processes might have to change, to use the system, or for other reasons.

Ask yourself "What else will we need?". Don't forget to analyse the requirements for things like documentation, training and help, preferably at the same time. Start to think about the likely support structure, hardware requirements and service levels. However, don't assume that just because you have identified a need *you* must satisfy it: the scope of the system defines what you are responsible for, and anything else must be negotiated (and handled under change control).

How Do I Document Requirements Using Use Cases?

Use Cases are the main way to express user requirements. They show *Actors* (user types or roles such as "customer") interacting with the system to achieve a required effect (or "*goal*"). Actors may include other computer systems.

The following example for a simple eCommerce system shows how the actors and use cases are modelled in UML:

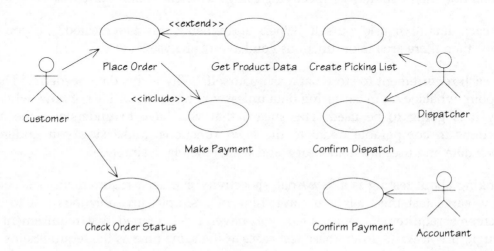

Each use case describes an interaction with the system (e.g. "Place Order"), which ends when the goal is achieved or abandoned (e.g. the order is confirmed), or responsibility passes to another actor or system (e.g. to pack and ship the order). A use case can include a lower-level one, or one use case can extend another with optional interactions, like "Get Product Data" in the above example.

A use case presents one or more "scenarios", different things that can happen in the course of the interaction with the system. For the "Place Order" use case in our example, the main flow documents what happens when all items are in stock and the payment is accepted. Other scenarios document what happens when an item is out of stock or the payment is refused, for example.

You document the use case detail using structured text. Include descriptions of the goal and the primary actor (the one who starts the use case), any other actors, any assumptions, and the main flow as a sequence of numbered steps. Then document the alternative scenarios as variations in the step sequence. Finally, if there are important non-functional requirements, like timing, document these as well. Use a standard template for the text, something like the following:

```
Primary actor:    The Customer
Goal:             To place a confirmed order for goods
1.      Customer confirms his or her identity to the system
2.      Customer selects a product
3.      System confirms product availability and price
4.      Customer confirms quantity required
5.      Customer repeats steps 2-4 to add other products, or confirms that the order is complete
6.      Customer proceeds to Make a Payment (see separate use case)
7.      System confirms order accepted, and provides order number for customer reference
Extensions:
1a.     Customer is new to the ordering system
1a1.    Customer provides new registration details
3a.     Product is not available
4a.     Customer places order to be fulfilled when product is available
4b.     Product not available - customer abandons order. Use case ends
3b.     Customer requests further information via Get Product Data then returns at step 4
7a.     Make A Payment fails. Order is abandoned
Non-Functional:  Product availability information must return at step 2 within 3 seconds
```

Note that this doesn't say anything about *how* the use case will be implemented. The same process could describe several different systems, or even a telephone order line.

The arrows in use case diagrams do not show the flow of information, but can show a change of control. An "active" actor initiates a use case, and the arrow goes from the actor to the use case. "Passive" actors are affected by the use case, but do not initiate it - these are shown with an arrow from the use case to the actor.

To create your use case model:

✍ Identify the different users of the system, and their different roles,

✍ Identify significant user goals that the system will support,

✍ Document each use case using a structure like the example. Try to keep to a consistent level of detail. If you find yourself going into great detail for one step, this is probably a detail use case to "include",

✍ Review the model with the users. Users tend to like use cases, since they are written in understandable language and say exactly what the system will "do".

📖 *Writing Effective Use Cases* is probably the best book on this topic, and *UML Distilled* contains a good introduction.

How Does Thinking About Objects Help?

Instead of thinking about the data and functions separately, modern methods consider both the requirements and the system design in terms of "objects". This is "Object Orientation", or OO for short.

What is an object? An *object* is a person, place or thing of importance to your system. It can be physical (e.g. a car) or abstract (e.g. a rental term). Any object knows things (called *attributes* or *properties*), and can do things (called *operations* or *methods*). It may be easiest to think about the object in the first person, like the car object to the right:

A "Car" Object

An object is a single instance of a *class*. A class is the "template" or "specification" for all the objects of the same type. It describes the properties and methods for all such objects. In UML a class is shown as a rectangle with the class name, properties and methods in three sections:

An object must have *identity*, *state* (its properties) and *behaviour* (its methods) in order to exist (or be modelled by a class). An object's state (properties) can change, but not its class.

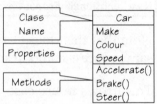

A "Car" Class in UML

Objects act for, or on, themselves. The car accelerates itself. Think about the object using phrases like "I can do this..." to understand each object's responsibilities.

Object modelling is made more powerful by three key concepts: *encapsulation, inheritance* and *polymorphism*.

Encapsulation is about hiding the details of how an object performs its methods. The object can have private data and functions which support the public interface - you can't see or use these. For example, you don't have to know about the inside of the engine to drive a car! UML allows you to model both the public and private aspects of a class. You show this on the model with "+" for public attributes and methods, and "-" for private ones.

Inheritance allows you to model *specialisation* ("type of") relationships. Children automatically *inherit* the methods and properties of the parent class, and can add others. For example, a general "vehicle" class expresses the common characteristics of all vehicles (e.g. they can all accelerate and brake), and then "car" and "truck" classes add more specific characteristics. Inheritance is shown in UML by creating a "relationship" (a line between two classes) with a triangular arrowhead.

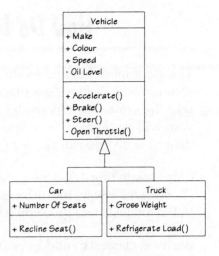

Inheritance is a powerful tool to model similarities and differences between objects, and later it helps you to share designs and re-use code.

Polymorphism describes where different classes support the same interfaces, even if the implementation of those interfaces is different. In our example, a sports car and a truck will both support the "accelerate" method (and a similar interface - the right-hand pedal), but the physical implementation will be quite different, and the effects may vary dramatically! Strictly speaking, polymorphism requires two or more classes to inherit from a common parent class so the common interface is guaranteed, but classes without a common parent can still expose similar properties and methods.

As well as inheritance, there are other ways in which objects can be related. An object can use the properties and methods of another class. This is an *association* relationship, shown as a solid line. One class can also be "part of" another. This is called *aggregation*, and is shown by a line with a diamond at the end attached to the "containing" class. You can model the relative numbers of each class. A special case of aggregation is called *composition*, shown like aggregation but with a filled diamond, where

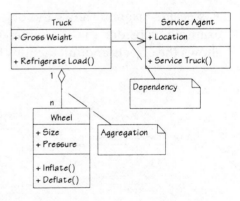

the contained objects have no independent existence. The example also shows how you can attach an explanatory note almost anywhere in a UML model.

Object modelling has several advantages. It models the problem in a way that relates to real-world objects and activities. The same model serves the analysts, architects, designers and developers and evolves over the life of the project, so there's no "mismatch" between stages. OO also allows and encourages good design and simpler code, and encapsulation (information hiding), inheritance and polymorphism all help to reduce complexity.

How Do I Develop the Class Model?

The class model describes the objects of interest for your system. During analysis, it should focus on business objects (like people and products). During design, you will take the same business model and add other classes that are system specific. Although you will only have a single class model, maintain separate analysis and design diagrams, so you can always present an analysis "view" of the system.

Class modelling takes place alongside use case analysis. It is natural to think about classes while working through scenarios which identify objects and responsibilities. Initial analysis will give you a first-cut class model to refine in the design process.

Business classes should have meaning for the users. To identify them, look for objects that have similar data, behaviour and means of identity - all objects in a class will have similar attributes and responsibilities. A class's name (a noun from the business) should be easy to choose if you've identified a relevant business object.

The public methods show what the class does. You can discover them by working through the use case scenarios. Each method should perform one easy to describe function. You then define attributes and private methods, as you need them to support the public methods.

A *sequence diagram* shows the objects that interact during a use case scenario. As an example, consider the eCommerce use cases on page 112. The following example shows the objects and interactions for the normal flow of "Place Order":

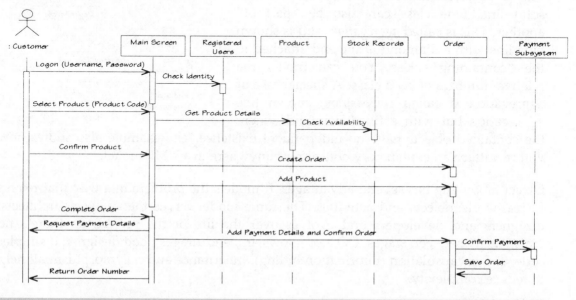

The next step is to try to identify classes for each object, and to turn the "messages" between the objects into methods on the classes. The class diagram to the right shows the key classes in our eCommerce system, after analysing the "Place Order" use case:

Note how I have added classes representing "collections" (such as a list of products), which have properties and methods related to the group of items.

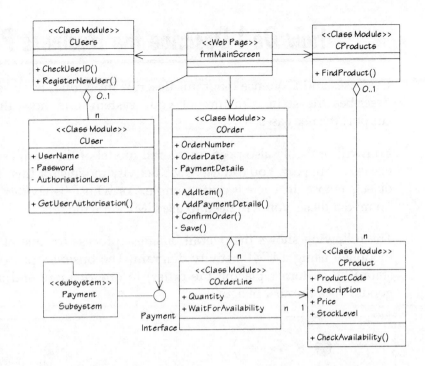

I've also added some private attributes and methods to support the public ones. Each class is "stereotyped" (using the << >> notation) to indicate what "sort" of class it is. At this stage, I have a *very* simple "design", a single "web page".

The payment subsystem is shown as a *package*. Packages are used to group items together in a UML model. The model can be organised by functional area, by use case, or following its architectural structure. The payment subsystem also exposes an *interface* (for handling payments), shown using the "lollipop" notation.

At the end of the analysis process, you should have scenario diagrams in terms of objects and messages, and "Business Service" class definitions. These express the required business behaviour, including descriptions of methods and relationships between the classes, but without design-related details. Where a database (or a design for one) already exists, you should also model this, as described on page 122.

You need to review your model for completeness, and beware of some common problems in class modelling. For example, if you have classes without responsibilities, one class collaborates with nearly all of the other classes, or you have the same responsibility within different classes, then your class model is not complete.

📖 This is a very brief introduction to the subject. If you're new to UML and class modelling, *UML Distilled* is probably a good place to go next.

How Do I Describe the Business Processes?

Use cases and sequence diagrams describe individual business tasks. The class model describes the static structure of your system, and how the classes collaborate to support the use cases.

You will probably also need an overall model of the business processes of which the use cases are part. You can use UML activity models for this. You may also have a few objects whose life cycle is quite complex, or whose behaviour changes with their state. To model these, you will need to use UML state models.

The following shows the overall business process for one of our eCommerce orders, modelled using a UML activity diagram. The business process proceeds from a start state (the customer placing the order) to one or more end states (e.g. receiving the goods) via a number of activities:

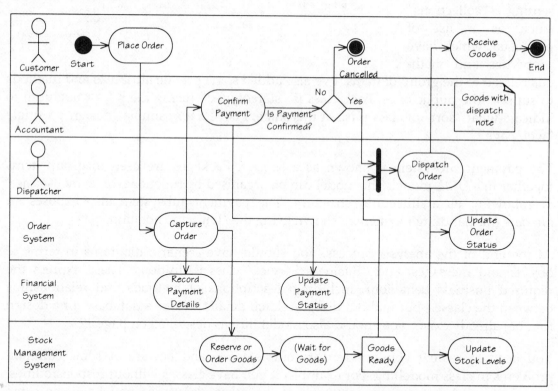

The activities are often grouped, as shown, into "swimlanes" which show the responsibilities of the various organisations (or roles) and systems involved in the process. You can model events (like stock arriving), decisions, "wait" states, and cases where several activities all have to complete before the process can proceed (for example, before the order can be dispatched).

Activity models also allow you to model an individual activity in terms of triggering events, inputs and outputs, or you can model the internal logic of a business activity as a flow diagram.

Some objects in your system may have quite complicated life cycles. These can be modelled using a UML State Diagram, which shows all the states an object can have, how it moves between states, and how it changes in response to external events. The following example shows what can happen to our order object:

The diagram shows the various states the order can be in. The lines show *transitions* from one state to another. They are labelled to describe the *event* which triggers the transition, and optionally a *guard condition* which must be met, and *actions* (non-interruptible processes that happen during the transition).

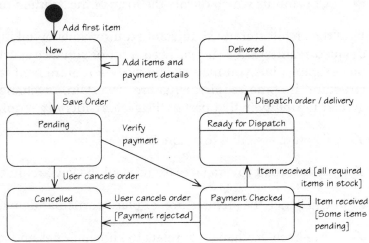

The label convention is *event [guard] / action* so it should be clear which is which.

More complicated State Diagrams can group individual states into "superstates", and can show concurrent transitions (for example, where the stock checking and payment checking are happening at the same time).

It is not usually necessary to model the life cycle of every object in your system. Concentrate on entities which either have a complex life cycle, or which are at the centre of complex processes. However, you do need to understand the events that cause each object to be created and destroyed.

📖 *Business Modeling with UML* is probably the best book on this subject. *UML Distilled* has good chapters on these techniques, and their more advanced variations. *Realizing e-Business With Components* includes a good overview of all the techniques, and is also very strong on business process modelling.

What are the "Architectural Requirements"?

The architectural requirements dictate how well your system must do things, some of its internal characteristics, and may dictate at least in part what the solution will be. They are *significant* requirements that can be split into three groups:

➡ "Typical" functional requirements for the "sort" of things the system must do,

➡ Quality and non-functional requirements, or *how well* the system must work,

➡ Constraints which dictate the form of the solution or the project.

Find the architecturally significant requirements by taking a "big picture" view of the detailed requirements. If you need a lot of similar reports, for example, then include one example, but you may also identify a requirement for a parameterised reporting structure. If some requirements are uncertain, or changing rapidly, then you need greater flexibility in that part of the system. Identify requirements which:

✓ Capture essential functionality,

✓ Have broad coverage, to exercise all the key architectural elements,

✓ Challenge the architecture, or place particular demands (e.g. for performance),

✓ Are likely to change, or relate to known issues and risks,

✓ Involve interfaces with other systems.

Don't forget "implicit" requirements such as printing capabilities. Other examples are auditing and licensing features, help, reporting, security and system management.

The non-functional requirements determine how well the system will satisfy its users, how it is developed, and how it will evolve in the future. These include:

✓ Usability (how easy the system is to learn and use),

✓ How easy the system is to configure, localise for different users, and support,

✓ Correctness, reliability and availability (whether the system gives the right answers, and whether it is available when required),

✓ Performance-related qualities such as transaction throughput and response time,

✔ The ability of the system to prevent or handle problems via security features and fault tolerance,

✔ Flexibility (to add unspecified future functionality, adapt to new technologies, provide components for re-use, or use components from other sources).

Your solution can be constrained by organisational standards, existing systems, elements of the solution decided in advance, or resource limits. These are all key architectural requirements. For example, you may have to use a specific database, or you may have limits on available bandwidth or memory.

Project resources and timescales also constrain the architecture. For example, you may have to deliver an early version of the system very quickly, but put in place a platform for more complex future developments.

Just like functional requirements, non-functional requirements and constraints must be prioritised, and you may have to negotiate if their impact is too high, or they conflict with one another. You need to understand the impact and cost of constraints and technical requirements. Choose where your system will excel, and where you might accept it doing less well.

Different stakeholders will have different priorities, and you may have to help resolve conflicts. A good start is to document all the conflicting requirements and their impacts, so that people can see the effect of their requests.

The architectural requirements determine the foundations of your system, and are often more important than any specific functional requirement. However, they are often overlooked because they are more difficult to gather. They are less visible to end-users. Analysts and users may be uncomfortable focusing on unfamiliar, more technical areas.

A systematic method can help. The best approach is to create a checklist of potential issues, and a structured list of questions which you can ask all the stakeholders: your customers, end-users, managers and those who'll support the system. A common problem is that this may appear too technical – you'll need to translate technical issues and options into their business effects.

Each use case should have a section for non-functional requirements, and you can use your checklist as a prompt. Avoid being too general. Focus on key transactions which really have performance requirements. Make sure all requirements are verifiable and ideally measurable.

You should also use "what if" scenarios to explore the system's robustness to future requirements and the ease of adapting it to changing technologies and user goals.

How and Why Should I Create a Data Model?

If the system is very data-oriented, you are following a data-oriented method or you are building on an existing database then you need to understand the data structure. If none of these apply but you are going to store data in a database you will still need the data model, but then it's really a design-time rather than an analysis task.

There are lot of ways to model a system's data structure. They use different diagramming conventions, and the detailed rules vary. However, most are some variant of the Entity-Relationship Diagram (ERD), which shows the various data elements and the relationships between them. ERDs are a good aid to understanding how data will be stored, and how data integrity will be maintained. If you're using UML you can create an equivalent diagram using a class model, for example:

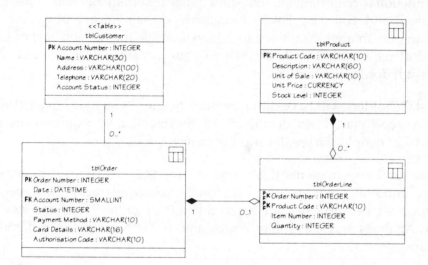

The relationships indicate each customer may have many orders, but each order relates to only one customer (for example). The filled diamonds on the lines indicate that an order line cannot exist independently of the appropriate product and order data. It should be possible to "read" a data model using sentences like *"Each ORDER must be placed by one and only one CUSTOMER"*.

You may show the *attributes* of each data element on the diagram (as in the example), but you will have to document them more fully elsewhere.

📖 This is a very brief introduction. *Database Design for Smarties* is an excellent introduction to using UML for data modelling, and there are more details on ERDs in *CASE*Method Entity Relationship Modelling*.

How Do I Document the Requirements?

Document the requirements by a combination of approaches:

1. Models describing the business processes and use cases, with textual details for each use case,

2. Models documenting the class and/or data structure,

3. Supporting text describing non-functional requirements and other details.

Models are compact and unambiguous, and allow cross-checking. However, they can't communicate quality and technical requirements, or problems with the existing system. These will determine whether a system with the right functions is actually acceptable to the users. You *must* use *both* approaches together.

The requirements must be as complete as possible. You may include preferences for the design, things like preferred screen and report layouts if these are known, or the results of prototyping exercises. You should include requirements which won't be implemented in early phases, but which constrain the architecture or indicate how the system may evolve.

The following are the "golden rules" for documenting functions:

✍ From interview notes, extract structured sentences detailing what is done in the business. Document the conditions (or external actions) that cause each event in the business, and how the business rules control what happens.

✍ Be precise with your use of language: use *must, should, could* and *won't* following the "MoSCoW" rules, and avoid other constructs.

✍ Avoid mentioning particular jobs, people, organisations or machines. In general, avoid describing particular mechanisms - the accent must be on *what* must be done, never on *how* it may be achieved, or *who* should perform the task.

✍ If a mechanism already exists and is being described, convert the mechanism to a description of its business logic. There may be mechanisms over which you have no control for legal or business reasons - document these as "constraints". Otherwise, the way in which you meet the requirements is negotiable.

✍ Requirements must be unambiguous, testable, and implementable. Check that there is a clear success indicator for each requirement. Think about tolerances: if the target response time is 10 seconds, but 12 will be acceptable, then say so.

Which Techniques Should I Use?

You may not have a great deal of choice. If for example, you are following a method like SSADM, you may have to produce certain models as deliverables. Similarly, if you are following one of the more formal object-oriented methods you will have to produce certain standard models. However, you will still have to make some decisions, and there's nothing to stop you using additional techniques if they give you a useful view on the problem that the standard techniques don't.

Alternatively, you may have much greater freedom over the techniques you employ (or even the method you follow). In this case, you need to be confident that you have chosen an appropriate set of techniques.

The first choice is probably whether to follow the object-oriented route, the data analysis route, or something different. If, for example, you're working in a real-time environment there are specialist methods and techniques which are much more suitable, and I wouldn't presume to try to advise you about them! If you're working in a standard commercial data processing environment, the choices are quite clear:

Ω   If you're working in an object-oriented development environment, then you will almost certainly use UML and object-oriented analysis (OOA). However, you might decide to supplement it with entity-relationship modelling if you also have to design a back-end database.

Ω   Even if you're not working in a mainly object-oriented environment, you might want to follow the OOA route. For example, you may have a few central objects with very complex behaviour (such as financial instruments), and you may want to encapsulate their data and processing in order to present a cleaner interface to the outside world. Or you might be working in a client-server environment where different layers of the system will be developed separately. An OOA approach is valid in any of these cases, even if you don't use OO tools.

Ω   Otherwise, if you're working with standard third or fourth-generation languages and databases, you will probably want to stick to traditional methods of data and functional analysis.

Make sure that you have a set of methods which complement each other. I've already mentioned the "Three degrees of freedom" for a system's behaviour. You need to make sure that the chosen methods will define the system's functions, data structure, and the way in which the data changes over time or in response to events. There are cases where one or other of these is fairly trivial, but in most cases it's better to be safe than sorry and make sure you have understood all three aspects of the requirements.

You must develop the different views together in a balanced way. If you focus on one dimension to the exclusion of the others you will end up with a very poor design. Take the UML methods as an example:

- If you record all you know about the business domain in a class model before going through the discipline of use case analysis, this may lead to a very data-centric model. It is better to think first about goals, then object responsibilities, and then the attributes needed to support these,

- If you focus on use case analysis without developing the class and process models at the same time, you may split the business objects up across lots of small classes with only a few methods each. Such a class model will lead to an inefficient and inflexible design, and more difficult development than necessary.

A related group of techniques (such as UML) provides for cross-checks between the techniques, to ensure that the various views of the system are consistent. For example every message in each scenario should correspond to a method on a class, and every state transition should correspond to a use case scenario. You should also check how each class's state is populated before it is used.

The trick is to get to a reasonable state of completion, then switch to another technique and do a lot of cross-checking, with the aim of finding omissions and going back to update the other diagrams as required. Don't try to get one diagram "perfect" before starting the others: you'll find a situation of diminishing returns where extra effort on the first technique won't deliver much extra detail. Switching to another technique and then applying the effort in cross-checking will be much more productive.

Remember that the models are there to be *used* - they're not just deliverables you have to crank out to keep the QA people happy. The most important use is to communicate your understanding of the system to each other, and to the users. This means lots of discussion, and *using* reviews with the intention of checking the detail of the models, and finding errors to correct. Don't try to get the models signed off on the nod by people who don't understand them - this doesn't achieve anything!

If you have access to CASE tools, then start using them early. It's much easier to build, check and modify your models if you use such tools. If you don't have such tools, you must apply standards and change control to keep the paper model under control.

You may have several analysts or architects working on different parts of the system, or you may have interfaces to other systems which are being developed at the same time. If so, you need to make sure that all the work is consistent. To do this, you will build the individual models up into one overall model, under shared or central control.

What are the Risks During Strategy & Analysis?

A number of things can go wrong during the Analysis stage, any of which could seriously affect your chances of success later on. You need to understand the risks and, as with all risks, take steps to minimise them:

- A major change to the scope of the system may sneak in under the disguise of a clarification of an earlier high-level requirement. The only protection against this is to question each new requirement against your understanding of the system's scope. If the scope has to change, it must be with the explicit approval of your managers and users. Make sure they realise that this may change the costs and timescales for the system.

- The sheer number of minor changes to requirements may overwhelm your change control systems and make your estimates invalid. You have to keep control of what is happening, and you and your analysts have to maintain a mental picture of the overall requirements. Your main protection against this is to watch the scope (see the first point), and to enforce rigorous version control on the requirements documentation and models. Batch suggestions, changes and new information, get agreement to a batch, and then incorporate the details into the next version of the documentation.

  You should also resist pressure to create a definitive set of estimates for the rest of the project until the requirements are agreed. If you can't get agreement to this, then suggest that you take those requirements which are defined, group them into a first phase, and estimate that phase first.

- "Paralysis by analysis" is a related problem. The analysts keep analysing the requirements in more and more detail, and stop making progress to the next stage. To address this, break the work into phases, and use use cases to determine which aspects are most relevant to the current scope.

- The users may not understand the documented requirements. You must put a lot of effort into communicating the requirements to the users. If you want the users to work with the models, then allocate time to train them. Don't be afraid to ask questions or deliberately suggest contradictory views, in order to get them to express their understanding back to you. There is no substitute for face-to-face meetings.

- The users may understand the overall requirements, but not the phasing or priorities. You must seek clarification of every "must" and "should". If, for example, automated credit card checking is a "should", it would be quite reasonable not to deliver this in an early version of the system, but you would have to check that the users understood this.

- The requirements may grow beyond the capability of the solution and team proposed in the Strategy. Watch out for this! In particular, if a detailed requirement doesn't seem to be feasible within the overall approach described, then challenge it, and try to substitute a simpler requirement. This is a very common problem if you are seeking to employ a package as the basis of your solution - try to persuade the users not to be too restrictive, but to specify a set of options which you may have more chance of meeting. Challenge them to prove that any restrictions are demanded by basic business requirements, and the cost justified by the benefit to the business compared with other options.

- The users may refuse to formally approve and sign-off the requirements documentation. The answer to this is simple: don't do any more work until they do so. You will have to be strong! Again, phasing the requirements and getting agreement on something less contentious first may help. You will also reduce the risk if you spend time discussing earlier versions of the documentation and getting provisional agreement to them.

- You may have resourcing problems: either with staffing, or equipment and tools. The main defence is to make sure your requirements are clearly, formally and promptly expressed to your managers. It's a good idea to have contingency plans: alternative ways of working, or alternative staff profiles which may be acceptable - you can't predict what the problems will be.

Most of these risks are related to problems of communication. It is quite right for you to spend a good proportion of your time communicating the plan and requirements, and seeking confirmation that your managers and users have understood them.

The analysis is complete when you could build and test the system without further reference to the users (except perhaps on details of design such as style and layout). The best person to judge this is probably the designer, or one of the builders. Get them to review the document(s) and assess how much more detail they require.

Highlight, and document separately, any unresolved issues which prevent you completing the analysis. Make sure the users know which issues are causing problems and when you need them resolved. If you have to make working assumptions to proceed, make sure these are fully documented and accepted. If you cannot agree on working assumptions, then do not try to proceed any further with that area of the system. If the assumptions later prove to be wrong, make the corrections under proper change control - you may be able to modify the plan and budget if the change of assumption impacts significantly on the plan.

What Do I Deliver?

The following is a typical set of deliverables from Analysis:

▤   *Statement of Requirements*. This should be a formal, structured description of the business processes to be automated, and the functional, technical and quality requirements of the system which will do it. It must detail any assumptions or constraints which determine the solution, and must extend to any interfaces from the system to others. This may evolve from the Strategy documentation, but it is a separate document, with separate objectives. You must maintain it throughout the rest of the project. (See page 123 for details.)

▤   *Models*. These may be either appendices to the Statement of Requirements, supporting the textual requirements, or the core of the requirements, with textual details where required. The preference depends on the choice of techniques, the tools you have available, and the future structure of the project.

▤   Updated *Project Plan*. You should update this to complete the estimates and plan for the agreed requirements and approach, at least for Design and Build of the current phase. If you are using tools, techniques or technology which are unknown to you, either include a generous contingency, or propose to review the plan after a pilot to explore the tools you will use. In any case, you must maintain the plan and use it as the basis for progress monitoring and reporting.

▤   Updated *Quality Plan*, and *Risk Analysis*. *Project File* up-to-date with all the communications which have determined the evolution of the requirements.

▤   *Test Strategy*. You will define the general approach to software testing during Analysis. The tasks and responsibilities will become an important part of your plan. (See page 170 for details.)

▤   *Documentation Strategy*. Clarify the requirements and responsibilities for documentation, training and support, in the light of the detailed requirements for the system. These should form the basis of the *Documentation Strategy*. (See page 172 for details.)

📖   There are many good books on analysis methods. *Mastering the Requirements Process* is a good introduction to the requirements gathering process itself, and you can find further guidance in *Software Project Management* and *Principles of Software Engineering Management*. Specific techniques are described in *Introducing SSADM Version 4*, *UML Distilled*, *Writing Effective Use Cases*, *Business Modeling with UML* and *Realizing e-Business with Components*.

Procurement - Buying It In

Sometimes, you'll decide not to develop the whole system in-house. In that case, you'll need to procure all or part of it externally. You'll need to define what you want to purchase, choose a suitable supplier, and control the process so that what you want is actually delivered.

Typically, you will turn the requirements from the Analysis stage into an *Invitation to Tender* (ITT) and issue it to potential suppliers for their response. Hopefully, you'll choose a supplier and establish a contract with them, they'll do the development and deliver work to you.

There are a number of different forms the contract and development can take. You must choose an appropriate form, and make sure that the procedures you adopt are suited to it.

You then have a responsibility to test, accept (or reject) and integrate what the supplier delivers. You, as project manager, have various responsibilities including controlling the communications with the supplier, monitoring their progress and reporting on that progress as an integral part of the project reporting. The vital thing is to keep control - you must know what is happening, and understand why.

I've assumed that you work for the purchaser of the software. You may, instead, work for the supplier. In that case, your responsibilities are what we've defined in the rest of this book, but it's not a bad idea to read this chapter so you understand what your counterpart has to do, and how you fit into the process.

What's A Typical Procurement Process?

There are several reasons why you might want to procure something from outside your own organisation, including the following:

£   You may not have the skills or resources to develop the system yourselves,

£   You may want to supplement your skills with external resources but retain control of the development,

£   You may believe that there are good "package" solutions to your problems - you'd be daft to write your own word-processor, for example,

£   You may want to use an existing system either as a basis for development or as a prototype to further investigate the requirements.

You must understand *why* you are running the procurement, because that will affect its objectives and structure. If, for example, you have decided on a procurement because a package will be a cheap solution of known quality, then you will be quite within your rights to question the justification of user requests for "customisation" which could destroy those benefits.

If you are buying a system (or some part of one), the procurement process will follow a structure like that in the diagram. The Analysis stage will produce one or more documents which define what you require, you will find a suitable supplier, and establish a contract. The supplier will then either undertake his own development process, or sell you the products of an earlier development. You will have to monitor progress and control communications with the supplier.

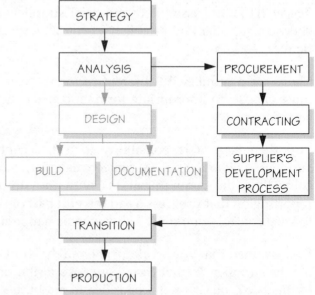

You will take this product into *Transition*, performing tests to accept it, integrating it with other systems, and preparing it for live use by the users.

If you are buying a service such as consultancy, the process is similar, but the specification will define what the supplier is going to do, and you will manage their tasks just like the other tasks within your project.

There are two central documents in a typical procurement process: the Invitation to Tender and the Contract. The *Invitation to Tender* (or ITT, also known as a Request for Proposals or RFP) is a document which presents the requirements, asks a number of questions about the prospective supplier's ability to deliver a solution, and the terms on which they are prepared to do business.

Most large organisations have a template or checklist for an ITT, and a defined process for issuing it and reviewing the responses (called Tenders, or Proposals). If not, then the following brief checklist for its contents may help:

1. Background to the procurement, and its objectives.
2. The functional, technical and quality requirements, derived from the Statement of Requirements.
3. Required deliverables from the development or supply, including support and maintenance services, training and documentation.
4. Required proposal format. It's quite common to suggest a format in which sections of the proposal match the sections of the ITT they answer.
5. Procedures for responding to the ITT, requesting clarification etc. This should include an indication of the selection criteria.
6. Expected type of contract and cost structure. Definition of the form in which prices should be quoted.
7. Qualifications of the supplier. Questions about their size, financial stability, development and quality practices etc.
8. Schedule for the submission of proposals, and their evaluation.

Make sure that the roles, responsibilities and dates in the ITT are sensible and clear. Ensure that the potential supplier can clearly see the timescales you are working to, the interfaces which you require between this system and others, and has some idea (possibly pessimistic) of your budget. Get absolute clarification from the users on mandatory and desirable requirements: if a package solution meets all the "musts" and relatively few of the "shoulds" it is a viable solution and the users should not expect to make many changes to it.

You will, hopefully, receive a number of responses to the ITT, and can select the one which best meets the overall objectives (but it need not be the best technical solution). You will then have to agree a contract with that supplier, and control their work through to acceptance.

What Are the Different Types of Procurement?

There are a number of different types of contract, which relate to different types of supply and project structures, including the following:

- A *Fixed Price* contract defines fairly precisely the products and services which the supplier will provide, and sets a fixed price for that work. It's particularly suitable if the work is well defined and the risk of failure is low. An example would be the supply and installation of a given number of copies of a package.

  If the work is less well defined then a fixed-price contract may still be agreed. This has the advantage (for the customer) of shifting the commercial risk squarely onto the supplier. In return, however, the supplier may have to apply a substantial contingency to his estimated costs. He will also take complete control of the development process, and the customer may have rather limited control over things like staffing and quality. Discussions over changes to the requirements may become quite contentious. Ultimately, if the requirements are too unclear, no sensible supplier will offer a fixed-price bid for the work.

- The alternative is a *Time and Materials* contract. In this, the supplier will agree to perform an agreed scope of work, using agreed resources, at a cost based on rates for the time spent, plus the costs of materials, machines and expenses.

  A time and materials contract shifts the commercial risk onto the customer. The supplier may not be penalised if he fails to meet time and budget constraints, and will have little incentive to reject changes. For this reason, the customer should take much greater control of the project, possibly to the extent of having the supplier personnel working directly under his management.

- A *Consultancy Contract* is a variant on this for the services of named specialists, usually working directly under customer management.

- A *Maintenance Contract* (there are other names for this) states that the supplier will maintain some items of hardware or software, providing support and rectification of problems, usually for a fixed annual fee.

The decision on the form of contract is an important one for your organisation, and must be made by senior management, taking legal or commercial advice if necessary. You must understand the risks and benefits associated with each form of contract, and provide advice if required. In general, a fixed-price contract is better for the customer, but you must consider the true state of the requirements and the technical risks.

Another factor to consider is the form of the solution. There are five main variants, placing progressively more control (and responsibility) in the hands of the customer:

   ❧   A *Turnkey* system is one in which the supplier provides software (and possibly hardware), and takes full responsibility for installation, support and so on.

   ❧   A *Package* solution is one where the supplier provides components of the solution, but the customer takes responsibility for integrating these together, and may take much of the responsibility for installation and support. The supplier may provide help configuring and setting up the software.

   ❧   You may buy *components* or access to *services*, which you (or another supplier) combine into a larger solution. Commercially this is very similar to package procurement, but the scale and responsibilities may be different.

   ❧   The supplier may agree to supply a solution based on existing items, *customised* to meet specific customer requirements. Customising an underlying package is extremely risky, and you should avoid this unless the supplier can guarantee that they can still easily maintain and upgrade the system. You must strike a balance between meeting the ideal requirements, and controlling cost and risk.

   ❧   Finally, the supplier may develop a completely *bespoke* (custom) solution to the customer's requirements, possibly (but not necessarily) under the customer's direct control. The customer must fully specify the requirements, and take an active part in controlling and accepting the development.

The route you choose will depend whether any existing solution matches the requirements, the willingness of the supplier to undertake bespoke development, and the cost/benefit justification of any changes or development required to close the gap.

Who Drafts and Controls the Contract?

You should expect senior managers and their legal and commercial advisors (possibly a purchasing department) to do most of this. Leave the legal aspects in their hands - they will ask if they need you to make a decision. Concentrate on making sure the requirements are properly defined and documented. However, do ask to review the contract, check that you understand it, and challenge it (to your managers) if you think the terms are unreasonable.

A senior manager in your organisation will probably act as *contract manager*, with the authority to sign the contract and any variations to it. To ensure management control, the contract manager and project manager should not be the same person. You will therefore need to work with the contract manager to run and maintain the contract.

How Do I Choose the Right Supplier?

Selecting a software supplier isn't as simple as choosing the supplier with the lowest price, or even the product with the closest match to your requirements. Instead, you need to take a number of possibly conflicting factors into account, and find some way of coming up with a quantitative justification for one supplier over another.

Aim to get five or six full responses to your ITT. If you have many more tenders than this, it will take a long time to evaluate them and making a choice will be difficult. If you have a much smaller number you may not have sufficient choice. In practice, this means issuing the ITT to about eight potential suppliers. If there are many more than this you may have to prequalify them. If you cannot find this many your requirements may be too complex or restrictive. If you are trying to find a package this may suggest your requirements need a custom solution.

The first thing to do is evaluate the functional fit of each proposal. Check that each solution can meet all the mandatory requirements - you can probably reject any solution which doesn't (unless none of them do!). Then review how the requirements will be met. Some suppliers may be proposing a custom software development to exactly meet your requirements (but with an attendant risk), while others will be proposing a package (possibly customised) which will have a lower risk, but a less good match. Go through your requirements, and score each proposal 10 if it can meet the requirement directly, 5 if it needs customisation or new development, and 0 if it can't meet the requirement at all. You can make this more sophisticated if you want to. Total up the scores, and you have a value for "weighted functional fit".

Now check that you are comparing like with like in respect of the costs. Ideally, all the suppliers will have bid in the format you requested, but this isn't always the case. You may need to either get them to re-bid against a fixed cost structure, or interpret and modify their figures to get a better comparison.

Can the supplier deliver what they promise? Will they still be around to support your system in a few years' time? Get copies of their last three years' accounts, and get your accountant to look at them. How big is the supplier's organisation? Will they be overloaded by your work, and have to grow rapidly to meet your requirements? Or are they underworked at present and completely dependent on your custom?

You also need to investigate the supplier's approach to quality. Ask appropriate questions in your ITT, but be prepared to make or commission a quality audit at the supplier's site. The questions to ask include:

? Do they have a development method and standards? Is there documentary evidence of this?
? What is the technical documentation for the system like? Is the code properly structured and documented?
? How will the software be supported, and how are problems handled?
? Is there good change and configuration management?
? Can he supply or support older versions of the software if necessary?
? How good is the testing policy? Can you see the testing records?
? How dependent is the supplier on a few key personnel?
? Does the supplier put reasonable resources into staff training and R&D?
? How prepared is he to meet your contractual and cost structure?

Convene a selection meeting. This should include yourself, the users, your managers, and any others involved in the procurement process. Each should review the tenders, and then hold the meeting to review the factors discussed above. Agree the scores and weighting for each factor, then work out weighted totals as follows:

Aspect of Tender	Weighting	Supplier A	Supplier B	Supplier C
Weighted Functional Fit	10	6	4	5
Cost (=£100 000/quoted total)	5	3	4	3
Financial stability	5	3	6	6
Ability to meet workload	3	3	6	6
Ability to meet schedule	5	6	3	5
Quality Practices	7	5	5	4
Contractual stance	2	7	3	7
WEIGHTED TOTALS		178	164	180

This will narrow the short-list down to two or three. You can then subject this short-list to further review. You can request clarification on commercial, functional or quality aspects if necessary. Perform the quality audits if you haven't already done so. It is a good idea to arrange a demonstration on the supplier premises, and possibly to visit reference sites.

A second selection meeting will usually confirm a first and second choice supplier. You can then start to negotiate the contract with your first choice supplier. If time is tight, you may need to issue a limited *Instruction to Proceed* of lower value than the contract but allowing work to continue while the contract is agreed and signed. You can inform the unsuccessful tenderers, but it's a good idea to keep the option of the second placed supplier open until the contract is established.

How Do I Control the Supplier?

If it's important to monitor and report on the progress of tasks within your team, it's even more vital to check the progress of a supplier. If he fails to meet his obligations (or if you fail to meet yours to him), then the dispute could become a legal one. The problem is that you won't have so much control over the supplier's activities, and the supplier may be tempted to hide or belittle problems affecting his work.

There are four essential elements so you can control a contract:

1. A clear, comprehensive and precise statement of requirements.

2. A series of clear, scheduled and testable (or reviewable) deliverables.

3. Formalised communications between the two project managers.

4. Change control: any changes to the requirements, plan or contract must be properly justified and authorised, and you must know *exactly* which requirements each version of the documentation or software meets.

If you don't have the first at ITT time, then get it as soon as you can! Spend some time at the beginning of the contract with the supplier and the users making sure that you have a document which you all understand, and agree as the basis of the work the supplier will do. Refer to this from the signed contract, and note that it will therefore take priority over earlier documents.

Make sure the supplier has lots of regular, clear deliverables. It's a good idea to link stage payments to particular deliverables - the supplier will then make sure that you get these, on time if at all possible! They will give a clear indication of progress, and may actually give you something useful early on. Definitely *don't* accept a contract which essentially says "we'll go away and come back in two years with the answer" - two years' time is far too late to find out there are problems!

Ensure that all communications are between the two project managers, and properly documented. Remember - if you have to go to court, your memory of a spoken communication is much less reliable than a copy of a written one. Create special Project Event Communication forms for this purpose, and use them to document every exchange between the two teams.

Make sure both project managers complete regular formal progress reports, and review them at regular progress meetings. These should involve senior managers from each side, so that there can be no excuses if corrective actions aren't carried out. You should take the responsibility for writing the minutes of these meetings.

Any change to a contract is expensive, and may change the commercial terms or timescales. The requirements must be as correct and complete as possible. Work within the agreed scope, and make a minimum of further changes, under strict control. The budget holder must properly authorise *every* change, and you must understand the business justification for it. Make sure the users understand the impact on the system as a whole. Don't allow an environment in which changes can be made rapidly on a user whim - this will create a growing stream of changes outside anyone's control, which will almost certainly result in contractual difficulties.

You must check the deliverables when they arrive - there will be a lot of pressure on the supplier to give you *something* so payment will be authorised, and quality might sometimes suffer. Accepting things is usually a two-stage process. The supplier delivers a deliverable, and you review or test it. If it fails these tests, it is rejected. If it passes, it then goes to second-stage acceptance which will also involve the users. The users must understand that their part of this process is vital and cannot be delegated.

What if the supplier fails to deliver?

The most common problem is that deliverables have an unacceptable number of errors. You must complete your testing as far as possible, and fully document all problems. There is nothing worse than rejecting the delivery at the first problem, getting that fixed and then rejecting it again only slightly further into the test process. Make sure that the supplier understands the nature of the problem, and has put in place both extra resources and changes to the way he does things which will correct the problems. This is his "recovery plan".

If the recovery plan fails or is unacceptable, you may have to change the contract. It is better to either reduce the scope (and price) of the job, or to adjust the timescales so that some things are phased for a later delivery. It is usually a bad move to accept some of the responsibilities for development yourself. However, you *will* need to do extra testing if you think there's a quality problem. Abandoning the contract is very much a last resort, and is unlikely except under extreme provocation. If this looks likely, be careful not to prejudice any discussion or negotiation, but try to get as much useful product from the project as possible.

If you detect *any* problem, then inform your managers as soon as possible - failure to do so could have serious commercial consequences. Try to find out the reasons for the problem, and look at possible solutions if you can think of any. Present these as well, and your managers should be able to make a quick but informed decision.

What Else do I Need to Check?

Is the Supplier Being Paid?

One of the most common sources of disagreement with a supplier is when he hasn't been paid for the work he has done. Sometimes, this is a deliberate decision on the part of the purchaser, who may be unhappy with the work. I don't recommend this as an approach - it's much more likely to reduce co-operation and create bad feeling than have any positive effect. However, if you feel that you *must* do this, then check your rights under the contract carefully, make sure you have all the possible evidence of any problems, and, most importantly, get senior management backing for the decision. Don't take such a decision on your own.

More often, payment problems mean that either the paperwork has got lost, or someone who should authorise payment hasn't done so. You must take responsibility for checking that this doesn't happen. As a starting point, it's a good idea to document how invoices and payments should be processed (a sort of life-cycle), and get this signed off by the various parties involved, like your accounts department. Make sure you understand the payment terms (like how soon you must pay after you receive the invoice). The contract will give you a good starting point on this. Review the contract and your plan, and list dates on which invoices should be issued and payments made. Then, set up a regular item for your monthly progress meetings when you can check what has actually happened, against this list.

If you do have problems, then make sure you have all the relevant details before trying to track things down. As a minimum, you must know things like contract and invoice numbers; who, when and to where the invoice was sent; any relevant account numbers and so on. If you can provide all this data, you'll probably find that the people responsible for processing the payment will be much happier to help.

What Happens to the Code and Documentation?

If you buy a house, it's yours to do with as you want. If you rent a house, then it belongs to the landlord, and you pay him for the use. Unfortunately, things aren't as simple as that in the world of software. This is because the ideas behind a computer program, and the source code and documentation, have a value quite independent of what is happening to any one copy of the program. The ideas, source code and documentation can be reused or resold. You must understand what the *Intellectual Property Rights* (IPRs) are for your system. The contract will usually define these. If not, get formal agreement as early as possible, *before* any problems arise.

There are a few common cases, although you may find that different rules apply to different parts of the software, or you have some sort of hybrid situation.

▢ The software belongs to the supplier. You have a *Licence to Use* the software, but it's still legally his property and you have no rights to sell or modify it. You have no access to the source code or a modifiable form of the documentation.

▢ The software belongs to the supplier, but he has modified it specifically for your use. Legally, it's still his property, but you may reach some other agreement about the parts which are specific to you (for example, documentation which is specific to your project may be your copyright). You'll have some access to the specific code and documentation, which the supplier may hand over to you.

▢ The software belongs to you. This is only usually the case if you've paid for a completely custom development. You have a right to sell or re-use the software as you wish. You may have a right to modify the software, but you may suspend this right if someone else (the supplier or a third party) remains responsible for the maintenance.

You must find out which applies in your case. The law is quite complicated in this area, and it's much simpler to have a proper contractual agreement. If you've got a more complex situation, you must agree a way of marking all items so that you can quickly identify which rules apply.

If you have direct access to the source code, make sure it's kept up-to-date, preferably in a proper configuration control system. If you don't receive the source code and original documentation for the system, you may want to get it placed in *escrow*. This is an agreement where a third party (e.g. the supplier's lawyers) holds a copy of the material, and could release it to you if the supplier goes out of business. If you set up such an agreement, it is your responsibility to check (regularly) that the material is relevant, useable and kept up-to-date.

The contract, licence and so on may also impose limitations on the way you can copy, move or use the software. Some will be to protect the supplier's interests (you will be expected to buy one copy per user of most PC packages, for example), and others for practical purposes (e.g. to make sure you only use the software on supported machines). Whatever they are, you must understand them, and challenge them if necessary before the contract is finalised. This is a good example of a case where the commercial people in your organisation will probably want your advice.

Once you have the software, you must make sure that your team and the users follow the rules. If they don't then it could be a criminal offence!

How Do I Work with an Unsigned Contract?

Unless everything is exceptionally well defined, you may have to start work without a fully signed contract. In some cases this period may last for a month or two. During this period, you are exposed to risks which the contract (when signed) will aim to limit, and you must try to manage and minimise these risks (see "How Do I Spot Problems?" on page 38). In particular, assess what will happen if the supplier:

❧ *doesn't deliver*. If the supplier is supposed to deliver something during the period of non-signature it is very difficult to impose any penalty or force creation of a recovery plan if he does not meet his targets. It very difficult to detect early slippage if the first planned deliverable is some way into the future. A good ploy here is to create a plan in which there are some definite early deliverables, and to insist on an immediate start to formal reporting and communication control. These will help you to monitor progress.

Remember, if the supplier cannot meet these early deliverables it may be an indication of longer-term problems, and it is easier to get out of the contract before you have signed it. Don't be afraid to flag up problems early, so that if a difficult decision must be taken, it can be taken while there is still time to correct the problems.

❧ *goes out of business*. The eventual contract will ensure that work in progress is delivered to you in the event of the supplier ceasing trading. It may also safeguard source code and so on under an escrow agreement. Make sure that at any time you have all the current analysis and technical documentation, and any custom source code (if you have the right to it). Clearly identify as your property anything you give or lend to the supplier. Make sure that you or a member of your team understand the work that has been done.

Limit your organisation's liability during this phase to an absolute minimum. If you can, keep the value of any initial payment or Instruction to Proceed down. *Don't* let the supplier take commercial or physical risks on your behalf - until liability is contractually defined any such risk could be passed straight back to you.

Don't give the supplier any reason to try to raise the price or shift the blame for failure. You *must* make *absolutely sure* that you discharge your responsibilities as if the contract is signed. Inform your managers of any problems. Practice rigorous change control, so that any change is fully approved. *Don't* try to use the period of non-signature to sneak changes into the specification - they will invariably cost a lot of money, and will be used as an excuse if there is a problem later.

What Do I Deliver?

Most of your (project management) deliverables are the same whether you have an internal or external team working on the project. These include the project plan, and regular progress reports. A procurement brings a number of extra deliverables associated with the selection of the supplier, and the creation and control of the contract:

- *Invitation to Tender*. This will comprise two parts: the requirements (which will derive from the Analysis stage deliverables), and the modified standard text (or "boilerplate") outlining things like the form of response, the commercial terms and so on. Your organisation's purchasing department may be able to supply the latter.

- *Proposals*. The proposals must be handled carefully. They contain commercially confidential information, and you must make sure that the fairness of the procurement process is assured. It's often a good idea to request separate "technical" and "commercial" proposals.

- *Contractual Correspondence*. This must include any product or proposal evaluations, meeting minutes and memoranda which document any decision. You must be able to show the process by which the final decision was made.

- *Contract(s)*. These will typically be drafted and held by someone else (e.g. the purchasing department), but you should have copies. Remember that these are living documents, in just the same way as your project plan. Make sure you also have copies of all correspondence related to the contract and any changes.

- Updated *Project Plan*, *Quality Plan*, and *Risk Analysis*. All three documents will have to be revised and re-approved when you know the form and plan for any procurement. The choice of supplier and solution may also mean revisions to the *Test Strategy* and *Documentation Strategy*.

- *Correspondence File*. This must include all communications with the supplier's project team, preferably on numbered forms. Change control is vital - all changes must be properly authorised and their impact (which may include the contract) assessed.

- *Software Project Management* contains a very useful chapter on the process of procurement, and further advice on many of the topics introduced here.

Architecture and Design

In Design, you establish a physical solution to satisfy the requirements identified in Analysis. Apart from an assessment that the proposed development is viable, you may not have worried about physical implementation before this point. Now you must create an architecture into which the different physical elements will fit, and define how each element will be constructed.

The role of the Design stage is often confused for two reasons: many developers cannot separate the logical analysis of requirements from the physical design, and have started to design their system during Analysis, while others may want to skip the structural part of Design and get down to coding. If you are in the former position, you must re-document your structure in the standard fashion - this will check that you haven't missed anything, and that your planned design is sensible and consistent. If you are in the latter position, **STOP!** It is very dangerous to try to build things without a properly defined structure, and you will almost certainly find yourself reworking them.

You should try to understand how the design is going to be used by the people who will build, test and maintain the system, so that the design documentation meets their needs. Ultimately, when the system is built, and it's being modified and maintained, the design documentation is arguably the most important of all. It's what most people will actually read to do their jobs. Skimping on it now (or even worse, postponing or ignoring proper documentation) will cause enormous problems later on!

Creating a good design requires knowledge of the tools and technology you will employ, a sound understanding of the requirements, and an understanding of good design principles. This chapter concentrates on that last element.

Why Do I Need A Design?

The importance of a good structure cannot be overstated. It is essential so that different programmers can understand how their product fits into the whole, and other teams (building interfaces or testing) and later maintainers can understand how the system is structured and where their efforts must be directed. A good design will ensure that all the elements of the structure have a similar style and operation, both visibly to the user, and "under the skin" to ease the work of the tester or maintainer.

The system probably *will* change in the future. You need to make sure that the design is sufficiently flexible so you can accommodate likely enhancements without major changes to the design. It is relatively easy to plan for changes and testing, and build assistance for these into the design. Conversely, without a proper structure, re-testing may be almost impossible and future changes very difficult.

The design documentation defines the structure and relationship of the build tasks. It defines the standards and guidelines which the programmers must follow. It explains how the different modules relate together, and how to interface between them. In some cases, you won't want to produce detailed specifications for every program. Instead you can define a "template" for all the related modules (e.g. all the simple reports), and then just document a few specifics in each case, all in the design documentation. In other cases, there will be complex separate specifications, but the design report will explain how these relate to each other.

In order to plan the build and test, you will need an "integration strategy" which defines how you will build the units up into the system, with corresponding testing. The aim is simple: you should gradually build onto a core which has been fully tested, and common components must be trusted by all their users. The developers and testers who perform this "integration" will base their work on the design.

You need to make sure your design fits into your organisation's overall architecture, and will interface cleanly with your other systems. Talk to other project teams and experts to get advice on this, and they can then participate in reviewing your design. Make sure you have some idea about how you will design the interfaces before you complete the design of the core system. It is no good having the greatest design in the world if you are going to cause problems with other systems.

Remember, your design may contain errors, omissions or weaknesses. If you document and review it properly, you have another chance to put things right.

What Are the Properties of a Good Design?

There are a number of characteristics displayed by a good design:

* *Clear structure*. It should be possible to visualise the structure as a whole, not just as a set of separate components.

* *Modularity and promotion of re-use*. There must be a clear division of functions into modules. If you require similar functions in two or more places, it's usually a good idea to provide one module which is shared.

* *Extensibility & adaptability*. It should be possible to add new functions, or change the details of existing functions, without significant changes to the overall design.

* *Resilience*. The software should respond in a planned, defined and graceful way to errors by the users or the rest of the system. As far as practical, all possible alternative inputs and failure modes should be identified and catered for.

* *Testability*. You should provide means to trace and time the execution of the system, providing support for testing and debugging.

* *Traceability*. It should be readily possible to relate functions provided by the system to the original requirements, and *vice-versa*.

* *A good architectural fit*. The system should fit well into the overall structure of systems within your organisation.

* *Simplicity & Economy*. As a general rule, simple, clean solutions are better than more complex ones. The design should avoid unnecessary frills, and you should challenge the requirements if the only possible solution is a very complex one.

* *Consistency of operation and structure*. Things should be designed and implemented the same way throughout the system. Examples include coding standards, module-module interfaces, elements of the data structure. A number of different approaches to solve one simple problem is a clear give-away that the system was designed by several people, or not really designed at all!

| Keep It Simple, Stupid! | Observe the **KISS** principle. In most cases, the simplest solution will be the most elegant, the cheapest, and best! |

What Does the Architect Do?

The architect (or lead designer) is one of the most important roles in your team. He or she is responsible for defining and maintaining the structure of the solution, and ensuring that it is able to meet the requirements. There are five main parts to this:

    ◐   *Understanding the requirements* - identifying the various stakeholders which the architecture must satisfy, helping to analyse the requirements and extracting those of architectural significance (see page 120),

    ◐   *Formulating the design* - creating a system structure which will meet the various requirements,

    ◐   *Communicating the architecture* - making sure that everyone understands the architecture. Different people have different viewpoints, so the architect has to present various views of the system appropriate to different audiences,

    ◐   *Supporting the developers* – making sure that the developers are able to realise the architecture, by a combination of mentoring and direct involvement,

    ◐   *Verifying the implementation* – ensuring the delivered system is consistent with the documented architecture, or modifying the architecture where necessary.

The architect defines the structure and organisation of the system. This is his main responsibility. The architecture describes the system's components, their responsibilities and interactions. A complex system is more than the sum of its parts. It must have a unifying, coherent structure. Therefore the architect must also define and describe:

    ✍   Metaphors, design principles and patterns on which the architecture is based,

    ✍   The technology, tools and standards which will be used,

    ✍   Key mechanisms, such as data access and error handling,

    ✍   Specifications and interfaces of components to be bought or built.

The architect will lead choosing the technology, and confirm that the choices are viable. He must therefore be aware of the alternatives and factors that choose between them, and understand what technical issues are key to the project's success.

The architecture must allow change and control complexity. To do this the architect may have to take the viewpoint of future users, developers and maintainers, extrapolating the requirements from the short term into the future.

The solution must meet the users' *needs*, but not necessarily every wish and constraint. The architect should help you to identify and resolve conflicting requirements, helping you to say "No", or "What do you really need?" if the requirements clash.

The architect is frequently an evangelist for new or different technologies, processes or solutions. However, he also has a responsibility to help manage change, which may mean reining in his enthusiasm where risks and costs would outweigh the benefits.

One of the architect's main jobs is communicating the architecture. He or she must become the solution's "champion", selling the vision and keeping it alive in the face of challenges. Each group of stakeholders needs to understand how the architecture meets their requirements. This requires multiple representations of the architecture directed at different parties. Architectural "reference models" (like the "4+1" view of UML, or the RM-ODP standards) define a coherent set of models and representations to meet the needs of most stakeholders, and you should use something like this as your guide.

An expert visualiser, good at abstracting and modelling solutions, the architect sees the "big picture", and views a system and its context as a set of interacting components. However, the architect must also be able to understand and discuss the system in terms of functionality, hardware, project or financial considerations.

The architect must help the developers understand the architecture, its value and the reasons behind it. He may act as a mentor or consultant, assisting, training and providing leadership to the developers. He may even work within the development team, focussing on implementation issues of particular architectural significance.

A good architect will be insightful, pragmatic, and able to negotiate between conflicting forces. He may act as a bridge between developers and management. The architecture will help you provide a structure for managing the development work.

The architect's ideas may be adapted and changed as the rest of the team adopts them. Conversely, the architect may have to adapt ideas originating elsewhere, but without losing the team's ownership of the solution. Maintaining the system's integrity through changes and the contributions of many developers is a major challenge.

The architect will often be responsible for verifying that the resulting system conforms to both the architecture and the key requirements. On a smaller project, where the architect is a member of the team, this may be informal, but on a larger project the architect will frequently run formal reviews of the detailed designs. The architect may also participate in or help to design and plan testing, paying particular attention to the non-functional behaviour.

What Goes Into the Design Report?

The Design Report communicates the architecture and design of the system to several technical audiences, including developers, maintainers, technical reviewers, and those responsible for the computing infrastructure. It should include the following:

1. The scope and objectives of the system.

2. References, and a description of related documentation and its location. Part of the documentation may be held in CASE tools. If so, describe where and how.

3. Assumptions, constraints and architecturally significant requirements. The architecture and high-level design are a response to these. Include any assumptions you have made about ambiguous requirements or "unresolved issues". Also include a Use Case model and introduction to the major business concepts.

4. A design overview. The first part explains the technical implications of the objectives and constraints, and then explains how the architecture meets the objectives, with any known strengths or weaknesses. An introduction to the architecture will include reference models (e.g. client-server with relational database), metaphors, standards adopted, impact of the project structure, and choices of toolset and underlying software (e.g. operating system and database).

   The next part is the logical component structure, which summarises the subsystems and their responsibilities. A good format is a UML package model with a paragraph or two of explanatory text for each subsystem.

   The component model describes physical components. A good format is a UML component diagram with some explanatory text.

   Physical models of the system may include a hardware model, showing host and client machines and major networking components, a deployment model, and threading or process control models and descriptions.

5. Discussions of specific design issues. This is a section-by-section description of the various subsystems and key design topics. Each should include some text explaining the main concepts, a diagram (such as a class model or Entity-Relationship diagram), and any patterns, reference models or other standard solutions you have adopted. Keep each less than 2 pages long, and refer to separate detailed documentation. The content of this section will vary, but you will usually include:

- How is the data structured? For example, you might include a summary of the database design, standard data values and life cycles of key items,

- How is data accessed? Describe any common data access routines,

- What is the structure of each subsystem, and any common components?

- How is the user interface designed? Describe the style guidelines, conventions, standards and technology. Explain if it uses a particular metaphor to guide the user, or there are standard features on all forms. Describe the policy on provision of help data and text.

- How are reports created?

- What interfaces does the system support, and how are they designed?

- How are errors and exceptions handled?

- What processes manage data as it grows over time? Are there any specific housekeeping or archiving features?

- How is the system secured, and how are user-specific functions and settings managed? Describe the structure of user accounts, menu roles and special accounts for administration and maintenance. Explain audit features such as check accounts and audit trails.

- How does the design support testing? Are there any special features so you can control or observe system behaviour under test?

- How do you control the system's configuration? How do you build and deliver it? Describe naming conventions, source code location and directory structures, libraries and other shared resources, and conventions for version marking or indicating changes. List configuration control and build tools.

- What are the programming standards?

- What resources will the system need to run? What are the performance, sizing, and resource usage estimates?

- How does the system support more than one language and country?

- How does the design allow for changes in the future?

Keep the top-level design document quite short and easy to read. Remember that design applies to documents too! Think carefully about the structure of the technical documentation, with the aim of easing the job of a maintainer who needs to understand a strange system. Think about what user documentation is going to be created and how it will be delivered. Aim to match the structure of the system and the documentation, as this will help readers find their way around.

How Does the Design Relate to the Analysis Model?

In some traditional methods focussed on the database, the models produced by the design process are very different from those produced by analysis. These methods require the designer to re-interpret the analysis models with tools closer to the physical design, which can sometimes be a source of confusion. If you are using this sort of method, the key is *traceability* – using careful, systematic methods to interpret the analysis, and making sure that you can always identify which design aspects relate to which requirements, and vice-versa.

The problem is less significant in modern object-oriented methods. Here, the design model is derived from the analysis model by a process called "elaboration" – the same model is progressively made more "elaborate" by adding design level detail:

✓   Design and implementation detail for the business classes identified in analysis,

✓   A data structure for class data you need to store (persist), and a defined mapping between the analysis level view of the data and the physical structure. You will typically also define classes which interface between the business classes and the data structure supporting complex queries, updates, and data-intensive processing,

✓   Implementation-specific classes such as collections to manage one-to-many relationships between classes, and "Key mechanism" elements such as data access and error handling. You may need to add members to business classes, and add standard supporting classes to the model,

✓   User service classes, which define the interface between the user and the system,

✓   "Physical" scenario diagrams, which express the processes in terms of the defined classes and their methods.

The elaboration process is iterative - you will typically add some class detail, then try to create a physical scenario diagram, which will prompt you to add other implementation classes or details.

To complete the Business Class definitions, you need to:

✓   Look for things which are common between classes, or optional, and where appropriate define abstract classes or inheritance relationships,

✓   Make sure that the following are defined for each class:

- All the public methods and the main private methods,
- All properties,
- Class-to-class relationships, their multiplicity and any special conditions,

✓ Add "design time" properties or methods needed to meet the programming language standards, support key mechanisms or manage objects.

In most cases, you won't design the user interface using the modelling tool, but you should try to express its behaviour in terms of the visible properties and functions it can perform (on user request).

You can check the class model by building up "physical" versions of the scenario diagrams. If at analysis time you created models in terms of objects and messages, you now need to convert these to method calls on defined classes, and add detail relating to physical interactions between the classes when they are implemented. You may have to enhance the class model with new methods and support classes as you go through this process.

In a complete design, you must understand and show:

✓ How each object is created or populated, and when and how objects are destroyed, if that is important,

✓ Whether, when and how objects are written to persistent storage,

✓ Any unusual interactions: asynchronous, event-driven or call-back mechanisms.

When is the Design Complete?

The design is complete when you have defined, documented and reviewed:

✓ The business and support classes, expressing and supporting the required business and technical behaviour of the system. Include the type and length of all properties (public and private), the parameters and return value of every method, and details of any algorithms,

✓ Relationships between the classes, showing multiplicity, guard conditions etc.,

✓ Database classes, providing persistent storage for the model, and the classes which add, retrieve and update that storage,

✓ The high-level user interface classes.

📖 *UML Distilled* provides a good overview of the elaboration process.

How Do I Create a Good Design?

This isn't a specialist book about design, and a lot will depend on the tools and technology you're working with. However, I can give you a few basic principles. Over the next few pages, I introduce a number of powerful ideas to help develop and improve your design.

There are lots of good sources of more specific design guidance. Use them!

- Colleagues and friends who've used the environment before
- Specialist books and magazines
- User groups and newsgroups
- Training courses and seminars run by the tool vendors
- Standards and guidelines introduced by tool vendors or standards bodies
- Vendor support programmes and knowledge bases

How Do I Aim for Simplicity?

A good design is usually simple and "elegant", with a clear structure and few rules to remember. The trick is to look for patterns which may imply an underlying structure. These can sometimes be missed or hidden by an analysis using the users' terminology.

As an example, I worked with someone who was designing a control system for a railway marshalling yard. The users talked about three different types of track section, and four different sorts of points, using different words for each. At the review, we realised that we could model this as "track sections", "points" plus some typing information. We redrew the analysis in this form, and ended up with a very simple design as a result.

"Simple" is not the same thing as "crude". The simplest data structure is probably normalised to third normal form. This *will* work, even if a skilled designer might then do some careful de-normalisation for performance reasons. However a database which has never been normalised will probably cause you endless problems.

How Do I Aim for Modularity?

A good design will be modular, and you should re-use common routines rather than creating multiple copies of a function. Think about the principle of "data hiding" (or *encapsulation*, in object-oriented terminology). For example, you can create subroutines that access the data, and insist (by standards and inspection) that the programmers use these to access the data rather than going direct. These routines can include integrity checks, the assignment of calculated values and so on. It's much better than coding these each time you need to perform each operation.

How Do I Get a Standard Look and Feel?

There are many benefits from standardising the look and feel of applications. If an application is internally consistent, users will be able to develop an expectation, or *conceptual model* of how the application behaves. They will be able to predict the behaviour of new functions, and the learning time for them will be reduced. If new applications adhere to, and reinforce the same conceptual model, users can transfer what they have learnt to new applications and predict how they behave, which will again reduce the amount of learning time.

During the 1980s, IBM developed a set of standards for human-computer interfaces, which have become the basis of the interface for most modern software. These are based on a few key principles, including:

☺   using *recognition* rather than memory, and menus instead of typed commands
☺   an *object-action* orientation, choosing the data first, and then the actions on it
☺   *ease of use*, rather than ease of learning
☺   a *tolerant* interface, putting the user in control and giving good visual feedback.

You should understand these principles, and the more detailed presentation rules which support them, as appropriate to your environment. It's a very good idea to create a "style guide" which explains to the developers how the principles are modified or interpreted in your particular environment. This should include things like standards for the screen layouts and menu structures, how data is selected, and how actions are started, stopped and controlled. Try to build up a plan of how the users will navigate around the data and functions, and reinforce this by a matching structure in the menus and documents.

There's more on making systems usable and flexible on pages 158 to 160.

Is There Anything Else?

Yes! Try to keep your design as pure as possible, but match it to the requirements, and note the compromises you make. For example, a design unnecessarily optimised for performance may be too difficult to maintain. Ease of learning features (e.g. providing lots of help all the time) could make an application more clumsy for frequent users. There will inevitably be some compromises in your design, and you should try to ensure that you maintain a consistent overall framework.

Why Should I Use Patterns and AntiPatterns?

Patterns are one of the most powerful weapons in your armoury, not just for the design process, but also for most other stages of a development project. Patterns are simply pieces of re-usable knowledge, documented in a standard way to be easy to find, understand and apply. They describe known, repeatable, proven solutions to common or recurring problems.

Patterns grew out of studies of building architecture, but they have been enthusiastically embraced by the IT industry. There are now all sorts of patterns: for analysis and business modelling, software architecture, design, programming, user interface design, the IT organisation and team structure, to name but a few!

Whenever you have a problem to solve, or you're trying to confirm that your solution is a good one, try looking at pattern books and web sites to see if anyone else has a pattern you can use. A pattern isn't a pattern until the solution has been shown to work three times, so a pattern-based solution comes with a strong recommendation.

You can also create your own patterns. They are powerful tools for communication, especially describing your design to other people. You may be able to show your design being composed of parts, each of which follows a named pattern, or your design may have a recurring feature which you want to explain to programmers or users. Patterns are an excellent way of doing this.

Patterns describe your system's architecture at a larger scale than individual classes, tables and so on. This helps you to manage and communicate a large or complex design, breaking it up into a smaller number of larger pieces. The patterns you have adopted also help predict the properties of your design, and the way it may meet non-functional requirements.

Collections of patterns often form a "pattern language" or "pattern system". The idea is that complete requirements or designs can be described in terms of patterns and their relationships. This is a powerful concept, very useful in the right situation.

An "Antipattern" is the opposite of a pattern. While patterns are about repeating the right solution, antipatterns are about things which often go wrong, how to spot them and how to fix them. These can be very helpful if you think there's something wrong with your design, or with your project, but you're not quite sure what.

There's no single standard for documenting patterns, and each book or web site does it slightly differently. This doesn't matter as long as you understand the pattern, why it is useful and how you might apply it. The core of a pattern is a description of the problem it solves and the solution, but patterns usually include most of the following sections:

Name	If each pattern has a good, recognisable name, you can describe your design using the pattern names. This is very useful if you use the same pattern many times, or you're trying to describe your design to someone who knows about patterns,
Aliases	Sometimes, the same pattern is known by different names,
Context	This describes the sort of situation in which the pattern occurs. This is useful when you're looking for patterns, but don't be afraid of trying to use patterns in other situations,
Problem	A pattern is a solution to a recurring problem, so this is a very important part of the pattern. The description may talk about *forces*, different and possibly conflicting requirements which you may be trying to balance,
Solution	This section describes the general form of the solution. In many cases this will just be text, but will often include models or sample code, especially for design and programming patterns,
Consequences	The pattern may have some side-effects, secondary benefits, or other implications. It's useful to understand these in advance,
Examples	A good pattern should include real-world examples of the problem and solution,
Implementation	The best patterns include guidelines on how to apply the pattern and make it work. This is very helpful if the pattern is for a particular programming language,
Variants	Quite often, the same basic pattern leads to a number of "variations on a theme". These can help you decide how to apply the pattern in a different context,
See Also	The pattern may refer to related patterns and antipatterns, and other material which may help you to understand and apply the pattern.

📖 There are lots of books about patterns. You can't go far wrong, but make sure the book describes each pattern in enough detail to be useful, that you can understand the examples, and the book doesn't waste too many pages just talking about how to write a pattern.

What Are Component, Layer and Service Architectures?

Components, layers and services are related architectural models. They are all ways of getting the benefits of good modularity throughout your design:

☺   *Separation of Concerns* – you split the system up into sections which different people, with different skills, can work on. For example, someone concentrates on the database design, and someone else focuses on the business rules,

☺   *Exchangeability* – you create a structure in which one part can be "swapped out" with another, as long as they both support the same interfaces. This makes maintenance a lot easier,

☺   *Separate Evolution* – parts of the system may change at different speeds. For example, the user interface may change very frequently, but the database design may be very stable. Because of exchangeability, they can change separately without affecting one another,

☺   *Portability* – you change some fundamental part of the system's technology. If all the technology-specific parts of your system are hidden behind a component's interface, then all you have to change is that component,

☺   *Hiding details and dependencies* – details, such as the ability to work with a number of different data sources, can be hidden behind a standard interface,

☺   *Reuse* – if part of the system does a job which many other systems or parts need, then a single component or service can be shared between them,

☺   *Sourcing flexibility* – you can obtain different parts of the system in different ways, as long as the interfaces are well defined. For example, you might build some yourself, procure others, and use a package solution for other parts.

In a *layered* architecture, the system is structured into a number of layers. Each layer provides a group of related services to the adjacent layers. For example, one layer might manage the data, and another layer might include all the business logic. A popular model for business systems has three or more layers (or "tiers"), managing the data, the business logic and the user interface (the "presentation layer").

A *component* is an executable piece of software which provides one or more functions to other software elements. The component has an *interface*, a set of method and property definitions which is quite independent of the component's implementation, so that more than one component can expose the same interface. The component will run in a specified *execution environment*, but otherwise doesn't have any dependencies unless they form part of the interface. For example, we might have an "orders" component which provides interfaces to add, update and retrieve orders.

Although the principles of components can be applied in most software environments, in practice a component-based system has to be built using an established object technology like COM, .NET, CORBA or Enterprise Java. You have to adopt Object-Oriented methods, with good tool support and strong models.

In a service-based architecture the focus is on individual method calls which a client (for example a component in one software system) can make to a service provider. Services, particularly *web services* using protocols like SOAP, can work across different technical environments, in contrast to components. For example, we might build our order processing system using .NET components, but call a credit card authorisation service across the Internet, without knowing how that service is implemented.

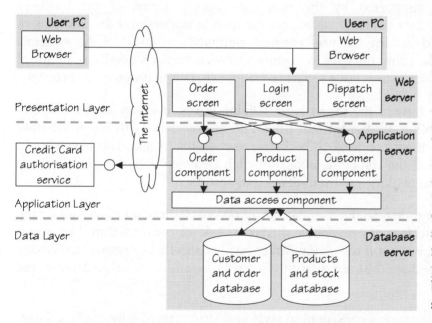

Modern systems will use most or all of these models. For example, the picture shows a possible architecture for our eCommerce system. The system is split into layers, with the application and presentation layers each made up of separate components. Credit card payment is handled by an external service.

You create component or service-based solutions by identifying the business processes, specifying the services required to support them, and then undertaking a process known as *"provisioning"*. Components can be purchased directly, provided by component-based package solutions, obtained by "wrapping" existing legacy systems, or developed to meet the specification.

📖 There are many good books on these subjects. *Realizing e-Business with Components*, *UML Components* and *IT Architectures and Middleware* are good starting points.

How Do I Make My System More Usable?

First, focus on your users' goals. The real goals are personal, not task related: "I want to do my job as easily as possible, not be too bored, and not make too many mistakes or look stupid." Then there are business goals, for example "I have to capture orders from customers." Keep both of these in mind – a program can meet the business goals but fail the personal goals, and it will be seen as clumsy, inefficient and frustrating.

Beware that the goals of different users and stakeholders may conflict. Consider an informative web site funded by advertising. Most users will just want to find what they're looking for as quickly as possible. The owners and sponsors will want to make sure that each user is exposed to an appropriate amount of advertising. You will have to balance these different goals.

Define the features supported by the user interface in terms of the business requirements and the user goals. Don't expect the user to understand the internals of the system, and avoid making the user express commands in terms of the system's structure. For example, allow the user to capture a new customer's details as a natural part of the order taking process, not a separate "reference data maintenance" process.

Avoid disrupting the flow of the user's work. Dialog boxes, message boxes, changes from one form to another all disrupt that flow, and an interface with fewer separate visible elements will therefore tend to be better and easier to use. The user should always be in control of the dialogue, able to switch between activities, and able to stop, cancel or suspend activities without disastrous results.

Make the interface forgiving, so the user can easily reverse their actions, and allow the user to explore without fear of irreversible mistakes. Ask for confirmation if an action is final or destructive, but not if the action can be easily cancelled or reversed. Provide *feedback*, with an immediate (but not disruptive), visual or audible confirmation of the user's actions.

Make sure the user interface is consistent in style and structure. Ideally, it should also echo real-world equivalents for the processes it supports. Armed with such a metaphor, and consistency, users develop an expectation, or *conceptual model* of how the application behaves, and can predict its behaviour. If new applications follow the same rules, users transfer what they have already learnt to reduce learning time.

With a *visual* interface the user can see, rather than recall, how to proceed. Provide a list of valid options from which the user can choose. If appropriate, support "direct manipulation" of a graphical representation of the business objects' state, but don't introduce complex techniques for their own sake. Keep your user interface appropriate to the user goals, and apply the KISS principle: "Keep It Simple, Stupid'.

Avoid *modal* designs, where the user must cancel an action before doing something else, or where an action has different results in different circumstances. This increases demands on the user's understanding, and may disrupt the flow of his work.

Allow the user to choose the data with which he wishes to work (the *object*), and then the *action* which he wishes to perform. This is known as an *object-action* orientation (or *data-centred* design). Restrict the actions available to ones appropriate to the object (*context-sensitivity*), and indicate the restriction of actions by context visually.

Depending on the users and their goals, the interface will be optimised either for *ease of use*, and learning by exploration, or *ease of learning*. Ease of learning features such as help messages at every step can become annoying to regular users. It is better to present help information on demand for applications in regular use.

Don't interrogate the user when an intelligent design can make this unnecessary. Extra confirmations, messages and "options" all interrupt work flow, and increase the demands the program places on the user instead of doing his work for him. Instead:

✓ Supply and use sensible defaults. For example, the "Print" command should not need the user to specify options for a simple, default print. There might be a fully configurable alternative, but its use is optional.

✓ Remember settings and choices based on what the user chose last time.

✓ Make actions cancel-able or undo-able. It is then safe to use default choices, safe in the knowledge that the user can fix things if the defaults weren't appropriate.

✓ Keep as much interaction as possible on the main window. Provide non-critical messages in a status area or via "tool-tips" instead of pop-up message boxes. Support editing in place, where the data is displayed, whenever possible.

Provide a manageable volume of information on the screen. Avoid the temptation to fill the screen up with information. If the user has to understand and review a set of data items, present between 5 and 9 items at a time. If you can, put the user in charge, and let her decide how much data to view at once.

In summary, focus on the user's goals, allow their flow of work to continue with the minimum of interruptions, be consistent, and you'll do a pretty good job.

📖 *About Face* is probably the best book on traditional user interface design.

How Do I Make My System More Flexible?

Change is inevitable. If your system is to last, it must be flexible. Sometimes being prepared for change may be even more important than meeting current requirements. It's impossible to make any system infinitely flexible, so you need to understand the nature of likely changes - being over-ambitious could damage your project too!

There are three main dimensions of flexibility:

๑   Changing functions, or *adaptability*,

๑   Changing workloads, or *scalability*,

๑   Changing working environment, or *portability*.

You may get some idea about expected flexibility when you interview users about their requirements. However, the requirements may be incomplete, mis-prioritised or change during the project. A more successful technique is "scenario planning", where you discuss the widest possible range of future scenarios for the business, and then think about how your system would change to meet them. You will have to translate between how the business may change, and the IT implications.

Your aim is to keep future options open, as long as that doesn't unduly impact your project's cost, complexity and risk. Try to design a structure in which the current choices can be changed later, but don't use this as an excuse to paralyse progress by refusing to make any decisions.

Don't tie things together too tightly. This "loose coupling" is particularly important where two items are at different stages of maturity, or are changing at different rates. Layered and component-based architectures help to separate things in this way, and you can change components with compatible interfaces. If you can adopt established standards for the component interfaces they will be more stable and easier to use.

Try to allow new or user-specific functionality to be added in separate, maintainable components. At all costs avoid modifying the core of a package system.

A flexible, maintainable building has "accessible services", for example running pipes and wires in raised floors and conduits. The software equivalent is to expose specific interfaces for configuration, management, test and diagnosis. Don't hide or constrain the underlying system software so that it prevents maintenance.

Make a deliberate effort in analysis to "find out what's common" rather than "find out what's different". This may suggest ways of improving flexibility, for example encapsulating business rules in a maintainable rule table, rather than hard-coding them. It may help to think of the data itself as "layered", separating the business rules, data validation rules, formatting information and data items themselves.

The most flexible systems provide a toolkit with which the users can solve a whole class of problems. The best such systems have a powerful Graphical User Interface, allowing "on-screen" direct manipulation of objects representing elements in the problem domain – this is the concept of "expressive systems".

Make sure your system has room to grow. If you can, avoid sizing hardware precisely to current usage levels. Make sure you can add extra capacity at a later date. Minimise built-in limits on growth: classical examples are restrictive coding schemes and hard-coded limits on sizing.

Flexible buildings tend to have very strong and high-quality basic structures, allowing change without endangering the building's integrity. In the same way prioritise the basic structure of your system (its architecture) over "finishing" (functional detail).

Don't be afraid to experiment to explore requirements, validate technologies and get new ideas. Make sure any experimentation is controlled, and can easily be stopped.

All stakeholders must understand that change happens. All strategies, plans and designs have to be living documents, responding to a changing situation. This is not necessarily a negative message – it can be an important tool to focus on the need for flexibility, on allowing for future change, and on sensible and timely prioritisation.

If the requirements are constantly changing, you may need models which represent "change over time", and alternative outcomes. Two documents will be very important: the scenarios for future development (ideally in both business and system terms), and a "roadmap" showing how the systems will evolve over time.

Flexibility doesn't happen by accident, it's the result of deliberate strategies. Where these impact on project cost, risk or timescale you need to get your users to acknowledge and support this. However, in many cases the ultimate cost will be no higher than an inflexible alternative. Flexibility is not a magic wand, but it can dramatically enhance the value of your system over time. The key to success is thinking ahead.

📖 *Expressive Systems* is very strong on how to build flexible systems. *The Art of the Long View* describes the scenario analysis method. *How Buildings Learn* is an inspiring book about how to make buildings flexible, with lots of lessons for IT.

How Do I Integrate My System With Others?

Your system must deliver the right functions, but it must also fit into an overall environment with other systems. How well it does this may mean the difference between success and failure. Your customers' business processes may involve several systems working together, and you may be responsible for integrating them. Your aim could be to ensure data consistency, support a process across system boundaries, or to provide a "composite application" using services from multiple systems.

Different types of integration have different requirements. It may be enough for two systems to share a database or exchange a file of updates once a day, but more and more business processes need the systems to communicate in real time. For example, e-Commerce will simply not work in some markets if stock information is out of date.

There are many different ways to integrate systems. The oldest way is to extract data from one system, transfer it as a file, and import it into another system. The problem is that this leads to duplicated data (which may be inconsistent), and can't support real-time integration. Another way is for multiple applications to share a common database. This is fine if they use the same technology, and you can arrange things so that you don't get conflicting updates, otherwise it may be difficult.

One system may call the methods or services of another system directly. If your systems have compatible technologies, this may be the best way. If they are different you will need to translate the request or event from the first system into a message, transport it to the second system, and translate the message back into a method call or database update for the second system. This is what commercial *Enterprise Application Integration* (EAI) software does.

EAI technologies make interfacing easier in two main ways. Firstly, the number of interfaces is reduced, as the interfaces are made with a central "hub", instead of "point-to-point":

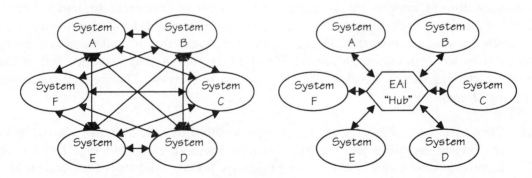

Secondly, you get a "toolkit" for building interfaces quickly and cheaply, and you might get pre-built interfaces to standard applications. The tools provide powerful mechanisms to ease common interfacing problems, such as transforming data from the format and structure needed by one system to a different structure for another system, or routing a message from one system to several recipients.

Creating interfaces in this way can extend the benefits of component-based architectures to existing systems which don't have them. You can use the data and functions of the old system in new ways, with an easier migration process to a new system.

EAI tools are built on industry standards for transactions between businesses. You can thus use the same technology for both internal and external interfaces, and possibly use standard data models for the interfaces.

If your systems use common technologies, the technical problems will be quite easy to solve. Your real problems will be managerial, for example defining the responsibilities of each system and team, and resolving different design decisions between systems.

You can design interfaces using UML. Model the data structure of the interface as a class model, and use sequence diagrams to model exchange protocols. You may also need to define the data structure and format or any files or messages. It is very important to identify responsibilities for specifying, building and using the interface.

Define when and how the interface is used, how the data will be validated, and what action will be taken in the result of errors. Security is important, so you must also define how to verify whether a user is allowed to perform a certain action, and if he is who he claims to be (authorisation and authentication). Describe how to operate and maintain the interface, timing constraints, restart and recovery processes.

A good interface design will be complete, so it can be used without knowing about "private" details of the systems. It should be modular, separating different aspects like security and each main function, and it should be extensible, so new functions can be added within the overall structure. Use a coherent and consistent set of techniques, and make sure the interface is safe, controllable and can be monitored.

If building a single system is like designing and building a house or office, integration is like "city planning". Each system satisfies a different requirement but communicates via shared infrastructure services, equivalent to the roads and other services in a city. You have to plan ahead, making sure that the infrastructure services (the integration tools) meet the needs of the users, and also that individual systems can connect to them easily. If you plan ahead for integration by providing good interfaces your system will have a much longer life before it becomes a "legacy".

What Are the Risks During Design?

Design is a very skilled activity, and depends on staff who know the chosen tools and technology in some detail, but who also have an appreciation of the wider picture. Whether or not you believe your designer has these skills, your design should be reviewed as widely as possible, involving resources from other projects, QA, technical specialists and even external experts if you can justify it. Remember - poor design decisions may not be immediately apparent, but will have a dramatic impact on your chance of success. Reviews are your main weapon against this.

Consider the staffing of the build stage as a constraint on the design. If you are not going to be able to get enough skilled programmers or testers with a knowledge of X, then you may have to choose a simpler design or different tools.

If you have to make do with development resources (people, space or equipment) which are less than ideal, then the end of design and the beginning of build are where you are really likely to feel it. Be prepared to look at all the options, and make sure that your processes of monitoring and review trap any drift in quality or progress.

Changes to the requirements may occur during design. As long as they are fairly few and well controlled, then you should be able to cope. Remember, your design should be both *extensible* and *adaptable*. However, you may find that the changes are significant, either in number or individual scope, and tend to bleed effort away from the main design activity. If this starts to happen, check to see if the analysis is adequate, or needs further work. If the analysis is OK, then get tough and refuse to process *any* changes until you have the basic design complete and documented. You can then process whole batches of changes together.

Invite the users to be involved in reviewing the design. However, you may find that they disagree with your planned implementation. A good strategy, combined with the use of design prototypes, should act to prevent this. If it fails, then remember that you (the design team) are the technical experts, and should be able to marshal technical arguments to support your stance.

It may be necessary at this stage to transfer the work between tools, environments or locations. This is always costly, and can cause problems. You should treat any such transfer as a project in its own right, with its own cost/benefit analysis and plan.

A big risk is to end the design work and start coding too early. Experience shows you will have to redo a lot of such work. Except for training and limited prototyping, coding before you've done a proper design is a complete waste of time. Don't do it!

What Do I Deliver?

Although it may be a shorter stage than some of the others, the deliverables from design are arguably the most important of the whole project. It is at this point, for example, that you can really complete the plan and the risk analysis. In a waterfall method, the design stage also precedes the maximum staffing on the project, and therefore the maximum costs and risks. Once the design is complete, the users will not be able to change the structure or style of the system, so it's important to get an interim sign-off on the high-level design and major design decisions, followed by a formal sign-off when everything's complete.

▤ *Design Report*. This is the main point of reference for most of the people working on the project from this point on. It must clearly communicate the structure of the design, and how to work with it. This document *must* be properly maintained through the rest of the project's life. See page 148 for details.

▤ *Elaborated Models and Program Specifications*. You will either create new design-level models, or elaborate the analysis models by adding design detail. Some modules may also need further specification, for example details of special algorithms.

▤ *Interface Definitions*. You need to both *analyse* and *design* interfaces. You may include them in the overall analysis and design documentation, but for the sake of compactness (and easy review by the other parties to the interfaces) you should usually separate them out.

▤ *Test Plan*, and *system test cases*. Create a plan which explains how and when you will test the software. Get the testers working at this stage to derive a set of system tests from the analysis, independent of the design. You can then cross-check these against the design to trap design errors before anything is built. It is critical to get the testing work underway early if you want a well-tested system.

▤ Updated *Project Plan, Quality Plan*, and *Risk Analysis*. All three documents will have to be revised and re-approved when you know the design and have confirmed how you are going to structure the build and testing. This may also mean revisions to the *Test Strategy* and *Documentation Strategy*.

📖 The sources of design advice were summarised on page 152. *Writing Solid Code* is worth reviewing before defining your coding standards. You will also find some good general advice in *The Mythical Man Month*, *Software Engineering Management* and *About Face*, among others.

Build, Document and Test

In the Build (or *Implementation*) process you create, test and document the system which you have specified and designed. It's very important to perform these three activities together, for all the management and planning reasons explained earlier, and so that you carry forward a product of known content and quality into the final stages.

The product of this process is not "code", it's *tested* code, and *documented* functions. The programmers must understand that they have a prime responsibility to trap the errors at source, rather than leaving them for the testers to uncover. They must also support the other activities, and you must plan and manage them.

It's important to set the right objectives for testing. You can't *prove* that the system "works", but you can *try to find errors,* and by finding and fixing them improve your confidence that the system will meet its requirements. The testing must be comprehensive, documented and repeatable. You should view it as a central part of an overall quality control process, which also employs inspections, reviews, walkthroughs and the efforts of the documenters, all to the same aim.

This is not a period of unbridled creativity. Keep to the agreed functions and design, and concentrate on controlling changes, keeping the existing deliverables up-to-date. Maintaining control of the configuration (the set of items which make up the whole system) is vital to ensure you can deliver the system to the later stages, and then maintain and adapt it.

If you are following a waterfall method, then during the build stage, more people will be working on your project than at any other time, using a wider range of tools and techniques, and on separate jobs. You must concentrate on achieving and maintaining good management control of all this.

How Do I Ensure the Code is Good?

On some projects, the programmers throw together something which looks like it just about works, and then "chuck it over the fence" to the testers. If the testers are good, they may find some of the bugs, but most of their efforts will be frustrated by low level problems which prevent them from running the more important tests. If the testers aren't much good (or if they don't exist!) then the users will find the bugs, which won't do much for their confidence or productive work.

The silly thing about this is that the programmers will spend more time tracking down and fixing bugs than they ever "saved" not doing the job properly, and the quality will *always* be dramatically worse than getting it right first time.

It is important to realise that bugs don't come from nowhere. *The developers put them in!* This is quite natural, but what you have to do is find ways of either preventing them in the first place, or trapping them at a very early stage. In analysis and design, we can use the techniques of discussion, modelling and review. There are related techniques for programming, and a number of more powerful approaches which can work wonders.

Try to create an environment in which your designers and programmers think about what causes errors, and how to prevent each cause. If you find an error which slips through the net, take the opportunity to discuss how to prevent it next time. The following is a very brief summary of techniques which programmers can employ, and you and the designers can enforce through the design and standards:

- If a run-time error occurs, the program must trap it, and report it to the user. Every time your code performs any action which could fail, such as accessing a database or calling a library function, check for an error. If one occurs, then handle it by displaying a message to the user, with as much location information as your language provides, so that it can be reported and located.

- Engage in defensive programming, but don't hide errors. Check for the "other" values and cases in each operation. Write code so you don't just ignore them, but use the error handler to show you something's wrong.

- Try to avoid things which are going to cause errors, or which are intrinsically risky. The programming standards may warn against certain practices: don't use them. Also, think about possible mis-understandings. For example, make sure that all your subroutines with similar parameters use the parameters in the same sequence.

- During development and testing, build in extra checks. Check the parameters passed to subroutines, and the return values passed back. Check algorithms by calculating things a different way as well. However, don't include all this in the version of the product which goes to the user. Use compiler directives to switch the extra code off, or just comment it out. Don't remove it altogether - you'll need it next time you change the program.

Your main weapon as a manager is a good design, and appropriate programming standards. These will embody the principles above, and explain how they should be interpreted in the programming languages you use. The standards should grow as the work progresses and you gain experience - encourage your developers and testers to think about improvements which will prevent each error they find.

However, none of this is any use if you don't *use* it, and *check* that it is being used. As project manager, you have to create and enforce a process of development which adopts these techniques and uses them. Make sure that every time a program is written or modified, it goes through some combination of the following:

- ☑ *Code inspection*. It has been proven, time and time again, that one of the most productive ways of finding errors in code is to inspect it. Get another programmer to check it against the standards and the specification. The "buddy system", or programming in pairs, is an easy way to do this without making inspections too formal.

- ☑ *Single step execution*. If your environment supports it, you could insist that the programmer single-steps through every routine when he writes or modifies it. This will rapidly uncover any problems due to the flow of control not being as expected. It will also encourage writing in short, well-defined modules.

- ☑ *Formal test*. The programmer should have his own unit tests, which he should execute *before* handing the work on to the specialist testers. It's not enough to think that the code should work - it must be the programmer's responsibility to check that it does.

You won't gain immediate acceptance of these techniques just by imposing them. You need to explain them, provide training, ensure that plans include them explicitly, and don't allow (or encourage) work to be rushed and the checks missed out. On a practical note, most people will do a job in the easiest way. A small investment in simple tools and templates (for example skeleton subroutines with all the error handling included) will dramatically improve the chance of acceptance.

- *Writing Solid Code* provides a lot more detail on these techniques. Read it, and encourage your designers and programmers to read it.

How Do I Do Good Testing?

You test throughout the system's life-cycle. The picture shows the "W model" of testing, and the testing activities you perform in parallel with the rest of development. Even at the early stages, you can "test" the requirements by preparing test cases and writing user documentation.

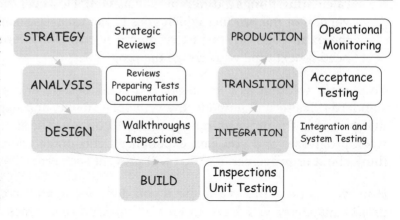

You build your system up from smaller units into larger ones, and at each stage you use particular types of testing to check each item. This approach raises your confidence that components have been tested in the appropriate way. The testing at the different stages is different. For example, you should check input validation at the unit test stage - if you don't do this then it will be difficult to do good quality system testing on the functions as a whole, because a lot of small errors will get in the way.

To do good testing, you also have to have the right objective. Testing is *not* about "making sure it works" - you can never do this (just like you can never prove a theory is right, only wrong). Instead, you should look for errors (there *will* be some!), and then check that they have been removed. As you find and remove errors, and it gets more difficult to find new ones, your confidence in the system will improve. You can then feel good about doing testing which finds errors. Otherwise, you will feel bad about finding errors, and you'll tend towards "proving it works", even if that's not justified.

There are a few key principles to make testing effective, efficient and worthwhile:

✓ Independent testers find more errors. Try to arrange to get things tested by someone other than their creator.

✓ Look for test cases which represent a whole group of similar conditions, or which test the boundaries between groups of conditions. This will increase the chance of finding errors with a smaller number of tests. Then check that your tests exercise all the code and the possible outcomes of each decision in the code (this is the *coverage* of the tests). What's left will suggest other useful test cases.

✓ Properly script all your testing - there must be a written or automated script which will allow the test to be re-run on another occasion.

✓ You must be able to show how the tests derive from the requirements and verify that the system tests have tested the required functions of the system. Number your tests *and* your requirements in some clear, structured fashion.

✓ Properly record all your testing. You must be able to show what testing you have done, and what the results were.

✓ Inspections are a good thing. It is quicker and cheaper to find errors by inspecting code rather than testing it. However, you still need to do the dynamic testing (actually running the programs) as well!

✓ There is no such thing as "code and unit test"! Coding is a quite separate process from unit testing, a formal test stage which should, preferably, be carried out by someone other than the program's developer. Plan and report these processes separately, as otherwise testing will tend to get confused with getting software working. A unit can only be truly tested when it is basically complete and could be handed to someone else to test. A good motto, which you should tattoo on the forehead of each programmer, is "Get it working, and *then* do a formal unit test".

✓ Testing is quite separate from debugging. Debugging is a job for the programmer. Testing should provide as much detail as possible to help the programmer track down and fix the problem.

Remember that you don't just do testing once. At the very least, you'll do it twice: once to find some errors, and once to check that they've been sorted out. In reality, you're likely to perform every test many times, because you'll find new errors once you get past the ones you found before, or you'll have to re-test after the software has been changed. This is why it's worth the effort of formally scripting your tests.

Regression errors are errors which turn up in software which was previously OK, after a change of some sort. They're caused by two things: "trivial" changes (and inadequate regression tests), or major changes to the software with failures of change or configuration control. You *must* re-test software whenever it's changed.

Typical code includes about three errors per 100 lines of code. Good inspections and unit tests should find about two per 100 lines of code, leaving one for the later test stages. You can quite reasonably set targets for your testers based on these statistics: if they don't find nearly so many, then either the code is very good, or the testing isn't. If they find lots more, then you need to review the quality of the code.

What About User Documentation?

The diagram shows the process of creating user documentation (in its usual relationship to the main development stages). Not surprisingly, it looks a lot like a miniature version of the main software development process. Documentation, like hardware or software, has to fit a defined need. The documentation strategy will tell you who the users are, to what purpose they'll put the documentation, and what documentation is thus required (and cost-justified). You need to analyse how the users will use the documentation when doing their jobs, and properly design the documentation so it meets those requirements. Only then can the documentation be drafted, reviewed, completed and distributed. Introducing the documentation should be part of the larger exercise of system implementation, so I've shown this as feeding into the transition stage.

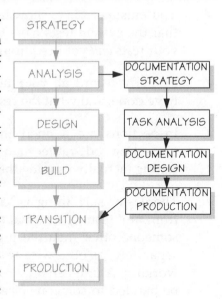

This diagram expands the box for "documentation" in the earlier diagrams. You produce *technical* documentation during every stage. You produce *user* documentation alongside the system during the build stage, but it has to be analysed, designed and planned, so the preparation starts much earlier than this.

When I use the term "documentation", I mean the whole set of materials provided for user guidance. These may include paper manuals, on-line help and training materials, among others. You should consider all the options during your documentation strategy, and specify a set of deliverables which is comprehensive but concise. At a minimum, it must include how to use the system, where to get help, and what to do if (or when!) things go wrong.

There are two principles which you should never break when writing user guides:

✓   *Write as you'd speak*. You should know who the intended audience is. Imagine that instead of writing to them, you are talking to them. Be grammatical, but remember that *communicating* is more important than grammatical perfection.

✓   *Keep it simple*. Complex subjects don't need complicated words or document structures. Write in a way that is easy to understand, without being patronising. Keep your sentences short and simple. Don't use more words than you need.

Good writing doesn't happen naturally. Start with a sound foundation which is well planned and factually correct. Write in a direct, instructional style, using short words and simple plain English. Review what you have written for clarity. Seek to remove ambiguous phrases or redundant words, and make sure paragraphs are short and to the point. Ensure consistency from one place to another. Improve the page or screen layout, and check for proper spelling and punctuation. The developers must review the document for factual accuracy, and the users must make sure it communicates what they need to know.

Hit Any Key to Continue!

As the manager of this process, don't assume that any spare resource can do the documentation. Some people are not competent writers, even if they are very good at another aspect of development. If you have access to specialist technical authors, or certain members of your team have shown good writing ability, then use them. A good technical author doesn't need specialist knowledge in the technology or business area. It's a mistake to "save" on user documentation: it's one of the most visible aspects by which your system will be judged acceptable or not. Bad documentation can make the system unusable, or cause errors in its use.

Make sure that all documents are properly analysed and designed. You need to have written specifications of what is required, and agree a practical and acceptable design. The design principles of "modularity" and "consistent interfaces" apply equally to documents as they do to programs.

Make sure every document is "tested", both by review and by comparison with the system it describes. Documents can be just as "buggy" as programs, and the results can be just the same. Just as with the code, the testing process must find errors, and provide adequate explanation of the problems to allow their correction.

Finally, just as with the code, standards are important. They will help the writers, and help the users to use the documentation. Standards can encourage good practices and discourage bad ones, and templates can embody a standardised structure for everyone to use. Make it simple for your authors, and the quality of documentation will be much higher.

📖 The best book on this topic is *How to Write Usable User Documentation*, which explains all these ideas in much more detail.

What is Configuration Management?

Configuration management is the task of keeping control of the various components which make up the system. At any one time, there may be several versions of the system (including those in development, test, and live use by one or more customers or user groups). Each of these will be built from different versions of the components. If you don't keep control, then the following are typical of the problems you will have:

- You won't be able to identify the source code you need to modify to fix a problem.

- Errors will be fixed, and will then recur because the wrong sources are recompiled into new releases of the system.

- You'll fix a problem in one version of the system, but the fix won't be propagated into other versions.

Your products include source and object code for the programs, the database structure and base data, the tests, the documentation and the correspondence associated with the project. At any time, anyone should be able to find out *what* exists and *where* it is stored, and preferably *which version* of the system each item relates to. It should also be possible to trace back the history of source code and documentation. Only by doing this will you prevent the unhappy situations above!

Your development environment will usually include a source code control tool (such as *SourceSafe*, or *sccs* under Unix). If so, use it! You can achieve configuration control without such a tool, but it's much more difficult.

The first step is to create a structure for the *baseline* - the set of files comprising the version currently under development, and archives of older versions. Arrange these under a common root (named to relate to your project), grouped to reflect the different components and other deliverables which make up your system.

Developers usually "check out" the current version of a file from baseline into their own working directory, change the file as required (and do their own testing), update the version and change control information, and then "check in" the modified version. You can then test and build using the new version, accessing the old versions if you need them. The source code control tool will automate the handling of the archive and the version information, and prevent more than one person updating a file at a time.

Maintain a separate copy of the built system and database for system testing, testing by users and other project teams, and live use by the users. When a version of the system has satisfied the tests in one of these areas, and the next area is ready for it, delivery is simply a matter of building the system from the sources and/or copying files into the next area. If you are using a source code control tool, it may be able to automate the process of building a system from its component files, and possibly also the delivery process.

Make sure every source document or file is marked with a version number. This will be updated either by the developer when it's changed, or by the source code control tool when it's merged back into the baseline. You should also allocate a version number to the system as a whole, each time it is delivered out of the "development" area.

The version numbers must be *visible* to users and developers. Each page of a document can show the version at the top or the bottom. The system can reveal its version, and the version of each component, on an "about" screen. If you make the format of the version information quite distinctive, you can also use a string search utility on the object files.

Describe the configuration as a whole, and the name and purpose of each file somewhere (typically in the Design Report). Anyone should be able to look at this single document and understand the directory structure, which files exist (and what they do), and where the documentation is stored.

As the project manager, ensure that your team understands and follows these rules and processes, without exception. Watch out for:

- 💣 Developers who don't put stuff under version control "because it's not finished yet", or who seek ways around the constraints of the source code control tools.

- 💣 Any temptation to work straight in the central development directories (or, worse, a version in test or live use) rather than following the process through.

Although there's often a "good reason" (usually "this is really urgent"), it's never enough given the problems it will cause you. It's much better to just follow the rules.

📖 See *Software Configuration Management* for a much fuller discussion of this topic.

Who is Responsible for Quality?

You are! *Everyone* has a responsibility to make sure that the project is following the agreed process and procedures, standards are being observed and what is being delivered will satisfy the documented requirements, without being over-engineered.

There is a great temptation to leave Quality Assurance to some external QA organisation who will somehow be able to detect and correct your mistakes. This just isn't so! The idea of QA is to establish rules and guidelines which will help you to do a better job, and then provide a *limited* amount of verification that you have done so. As project manager you have particular responsibility to make sure that your team is following the rules, and that what you are going to deliver is no more and no less than what has been agreed and approved.

It's important to spread this "responsibility for quality" down through your team. For example, your programmers must aim to prevent or catch errors themselves, so that they deliver as near to "bug free code" as possible. It's always more difficult and costly to remove errors than to aim for higher quality in the first place. Most developers are quite happy to strive for higher quality if there aren't too many conflicting constraints: your job is to remove these whenever possible.

Such constraints include the following. Watch out if any are true of your situation:

- There's no common objective, or too many different objectives and agendas.
- You don't allow for human failings and differences in your methods and plans.
- Productivity targets are expressed purely in numeric terms.
- The deadlines or budgets are unrealistic, or don't allow for quality checks, testing and documentation.
- Management won't fund or support adequate training.

What's My Role in Reviews and Audits?

One of your main responsibilities as a project manager is to assess, document and report your progress against the plan on a regular basis. Your managers, your users and possibly your QA group can then review this to check you are on track.

Resist the temptation to "dress up" the report to tell the reviewers what you think they want to hear. They would rather hear the bad news early, when there's plenty of time to react, than when the problem gets so bad you can't hide it any longer or correct it easily. Bad news will be better received if you can identify the problems and emphasise the options for improvements.

Reviews are your main way of checking document deliverables. "Checking" is a mixture of two processes: *verification* (have you built the system to its requirements?), and *validation* (are the requirements correct?, is the system worth it?). The mechanical processes of cross-checking and testing described throughout this book are mainly verification processes - you could conceivably be building the wrong system, albeit very well! You therefore need a validation process as well.

You can only achieve validation by describing the system (or its definition) to your users and managers, and getting their agreement. Do this by a formal process based on a review of a written document, as spoken agreements can be mis-understood or forgotten. It's therefore in your interest to document your work, schedule reviews, canvass for written comments if possible, and carefully minute any review meeting.

Make sure your architects, analysts and designers all participate in reviewing documents and change requests. The architect's "big picture" view of the project may be particularly useful spotting gaps, overlaps and inconsistencies.

You should respond to review comments indicating for each comment how you intend to react to it. Remember, it takes quite a lot of effort to properly review a document, and the comments are meant to be constructive, even if they reveal problems in your document or elsewhere in your project.

At various times, your project may be subject to an audit. This may be performed by your QA group, or by auditors internal or external to your organisation. In each case, the auditors will seek to establish that you have well defined, approved requirements and are developing a system to meet them, in a controlled and documented fashion. Your best insurance is undoubtedly a well-organised and complete project file, with everything in place and in order. Present the current status and structure of your project clearly and simply. Don't try to hide problems - they have a habit of revealing themselves whatever you do - but instead try to present any problems you have along with what you are doing to solve them.

Another key item in your defence (and a key component of any good system) is formal user acceptance of the work you have done. Strictly speaking, you shouldn't move from one phase to another without getting formal sign-off by the users, but there may be reasons why this doesn't happen in practice. The things you *must* get approval for are the Quality Plan, the Documentation and Test Strategies, the Statement of Requirements, major deliveries of the system and any user documentation. One good way to get approval is to send a memo direct to the user saying "Do you approve...?", to which a one line answer "Yes" is adequate. Don't forget to file both your letter and the response in the project file. Try to avoid approvals which are in meeting minutes - they can be difficult to locate, and if there is a problem someone may challenge the minutes as a fair record of what was said.

What are the "Best Practices" in the Build Stage?

Successful software development organisations often adopt a number of practices which help them to be effective and productive. Whatever your toolset and methods, you should consider whether you can share in these practices.

Developers can be very productive working together to develop a solution. The most extreme version of this is *pair programming*, in which the programmers always work in pairs. While one has the keyboard and is writing code, the other is reviewing and sanity checking the work. It's not just one person programming and another watching – the first is tactically designing a solution while the other has a chance to both spot errors (a process of continuous inspection) and think about more strategic issues:

?   Will this work?

?   Do we need other test cases?

?   Are there better options? Can we simplify/refactor this?

?   Does this fit the standards and the architecture?

You'll probably find that pair programming actually results in higher net productivity and higher code quality than solo programming, largely because every piece of code has been considered by two people, and inspected. However, if your team won't or can't adopt this practice, then consider getting a senior team member to review all modified code on a regular basis, say once a week. This is easy to do if you have a source code control system, and is not intrusive on the other developers.

Whether or not you do pair programming, you should allow time for senior team members to work closely with the junior ones, providing mentoring and guidance.

A combination of practices related to integration and testing can help to improve your confidence in the code, and means you always have a testable version of the system:

✓   Before each piece of code is written, you design one or more automated test cases to test the new or changed functions of the system. The tests must be automated, so they can be run repeatedly for low effort. Programming this way, writing the tests first, is more productive and builds your confidence, because you know when you can move onto the next problem.

✓   Build your tests up into an automated suite which exercises the main features of the system. This is not the same as a comprehensive system or integration test –

the types of test are different. The objective is to make sure that the system hangs together, to catch any gross errors, and ensure that things which are working don't stop working. This is often known as a "smoke test".

✓ Once a day (or more frequently) build the system up from the source code and other components. Then execute the automated tests. Get into the habit of re-integrating and testing the system immediately after any significant change, and the process will trap a range of errors when they are easiest to fix.

✓ Do make use of tools to help you detect potential errors. For example, switch on compiler warnings and use automated code checkers if you have them.

✓ Fix errors as you go. Don't store up faulty code to "fix later" – this sends out the wrong messages on quality, can have side effects on other work, and means you don't really know how long it will take to make the current version of the system stable.

Make sure you have good, agreed coding standards. If possible, use tools to enforce or automate them, so that the programmers follow the standards automatically, with the minimum of effort.

Continuously review the design throughout the build process. You may often spot opportunities to avoid or remove duplication, find a simpler solution or address known design weaknesses. Restructuring the code in this way is known as *refactoring*. Don't be afraid to model new ideas rather than leaping into code, and make sure you re-integrate and re-test after each change.

Programming and testing are fundamentally different from analysis, management and customer liaison processes. They demand a great level of concentration, and one of the most important contributions you can make to productivity and quality is to ensure the developers can work quietly and with the minimum of interruptions:

☯ Keep developers free from meetings, administration and other interruptions,

☯ Manage the level of customer involvement with the developers. You need enough to make sure you are delivering the right system, but too much can disrupt development progress,

☯ Create separate "talking" and "working" spaces. Discourage conversation (apart from short technical "question and answer" exchanges) in the working space – if anyone wants a longer conversation, it's time for them to get a cup of coffee.

📖 These practices are described further in *eXtreme Programming Explained*, *Refactoring* and *Debugging the Development Process*.

What's in the Project File?

You should maintain a file which contains all the communications with your project team, any documents which are only available in paper form, and up-to-date paper copies of working documents. Members of the project team and others can then use this for quick access to the documentation. In addition to the major deliverables from each stage (which you will probably hold separately and reference), it must contain:

1.   Change requests and associated communications

2.   Bug reports or "action requests" from the users or other project teams

3.   Minutes of meetings:
      • Formal project group meetings
      • Project team progress meetings
      • Reviews and Quality Assurance audits
      • Interviews and feedback sessions

4.   Correspondence:
      • Memos etc.
      • Review comments
      • User acceptance or rejection

5.   Plans and progress reports:
      • Overall project plan and other detailed plans
      • Regular progress reports if separate from the plan

6.   Test records:
      • Record of runs and results
      • Results of QA audits and code inspections

7.   Contractual Communications:
      • Orders and requisitions
      • Monthly Reports
      • Communications with external teams (separate from internal correspondence)

You *must* have a project file, and others *must* be able to use it without your guidance, otherwise you have not done your job! You must formalise *every* communication you have (particularly conversations with the users and suppliers). This is necessary to *prove* you are in control.

What Do I Deliver?

📄 *Working System*. You must test and document this in accordance with the appropriate strategies. Deliver it into the acceptance testing environment, together with a first draft of help text and manuals, ready for implementation or distribution.

📄 Updated *Design Report, Program Specifications* and *Interface Definitions*. Keep all design-related documents up-to-date during the build process, noting, in particular, any difference between the initial design and the "as built" situation. If you make changes to the functions during this stage, then you will also have to update the *Analysis Report* and test materials. It may also be a good idea to create a modified set of data models based on the "as built" structure, which will help communicate the actual structure of the system.

📄 *Build Instructions*. A set of instructions defining how to build, deliver and/or install the system, including a small set of tests to check the build or delivery.

📄 *Unit and system test scripts*. Create a set of written or automated test scripts (with appropriate test data) so that you can repeatedly test each unit, and the system as a whole against its requirements.

📄 *Project File*, including *Record of Test Runs and Results*, and log of all *Change* and *Action Requests* and associated correspondence. See page 180 for details.

📄 Draft *User Guide* and *Administrator's Guide*. Your team will draft these, and any other user or operator guidance materials, during the build stage, and complete them during the transition stage.

📄 *Provisional Implementation Plan*. There are a number of tasks during the next (transition) stage which require advance planning and careful co-ordination. You must prepare a first draft of this plan, so that you can begin to organise the required resources.

📄 Updated *Project Plan, Quality Plan*, and *Risk Analysis*. Review and revise all three documents regularly throughout this stage, in the light of progress, known problems and changing responsibilities. This may also mean revisions to the *Test Strategy* and *Documentation Strategy*.

📖 There are numerous relevant books, but *Writing Solid Code, How to Write Usable User Documentation* and *Software Project Management* are a good start.

The Transition Into Use

Your job isn't over when you've built and tested the system. You can't just dump it onto the users and expect them to get on with it - they will almost certainly refuse to do so. There are a large number of tasks which still need to be done, and which require both proper management and your team's knowledge of the system.

If the system's intended for a specific user group, then you may have to help with things like training, setting up base data, integrating the system with others, and testing the system in its live environment. If it's a system for sale, then your responsibilities may be different, but you will have to help set up installation routines and support structures, or provide help to the marketing and sales people.

You will have to make sure that the recipients of any delivery know what they should do with it, and monitor their activities to look for possible problems.

There may be a substantial job of testing still to be completed during this stage. In some cases, you will have produced part of a larger system, and will have to combine the systems together during the transition stage. In other cases, you will be procuring all or part of the system from outside, and will need to thoroughly test the supplied parts and integrate them into your environment.

The management challenges of the transition stage are quite different to those of earlier stages. Conflicting with the pressure to complete the job and get things working (which may be acute if there is slippage) will be pressure to "demobilise" and start to reduce staffing levels on the project. The transition stage tasks will involve a number of separate groups, and these tasks have to be managed, possibly by a specially appointed implementation manager, or possibly by you!

How Do I Move My System Into Production?

When your system goes into live use, it will place certain demands on the target machines and their operators. The system will have its own requirements for disk, memory and processor capacity. It will probably have to coexist or interact with other systems (with their own hardware requirements). There may be regular processes, such as backups, end-of-day processing or handling externally produced data which the operators will have to perform and verify.

You have to define these requirements. For a PC system, they will form part of the user documentation. For a larger system, you may have to liaise with the operators and managers of other systems to make sure everything works together. You may need to create a *production profile* for each system to standardise the documentation.

Define the disk, memory and processor requirements of your system. It's a good idea to think in terms of the minimum requirements (e.g. for a new installation), the typical usage of memory and processor power, the maximum volumes of data which the system can handle, and the impact on system performance of the maximum planned transaction load. You should also try to define how the requirements will grow as the system handles more users and data. If the volumes of data will become very large over time, you also need to define how to archive and remove older data.

If several systems interact in the live environment, you have to help define the *production cycle*. This is the sequence of regular events and operational tasks. For example, system A must do its end-of-day processing before system B can run a summary report on the data, and both must complete before the systems can be taken out-of-use and a backup made. These events must be started at midnight, and finished before the systems are required again at 7 a.m.

You need to know how long each task will take, and what to do if it goes wrong. If you're trying to get very high availability (e.g. to support 24-hours a day use) then planning these tasks can be quite complex. Use Case diagrams can show how the systems interact, activity diagrams can show the sequence of processing, and a Gantt Chart can be used to schedule the different jobs. (See pages 80 and 112-118.)

You need to document how the system interacts with components of other systems. For example, you may use functions, libraries or databases from other applications. This information will be important when delivering your system, or upgrading the others. It may also help the operators to partition applications between disks and processors. In any event, you may want to recompile your system in the live environment (and then retest) to make sure it works with the versions already there.

The backup process must take account of business and legal requirements (which may define how long data has to be stored), and whether the users may ever need to restore the system to a previous point in time. As well as defining the backup process, you must define how to recover from loss of the system, particularly when one of the production processes (on which others may depend) is interrupted. A good method is to create a *failure analysis table*, which lists the main steps in each process, and what to do if each step fails to complete.

You must define each task for the operators, and write a procedure for it. As well as the production tasks, this includes things like granting user access and creating accounts, if these are not controlled by the users themselves.

How Do I Test the Integrated System?

The "computer system" as understood by the users will probably consist of a number of elements. Some may be internally developed, others bought in. Some will be new, and others off the shelf. You now have to test that the overall solution will fulfil its requirements.

You may assume that each component has been subject to thorough unit and system testing, but this is not always the case. You will have to devise your own system tests for any component not created by your project: these should seek to check both that the item conforms to its requirements, and has already been properly tested. If you have procured the item from an external source, then these tests will form the *contractual acceptance tests*.

Having gained sufficient confidence in each item, you need to integrate them. You should devise a documented *integration strategy*, in which the items will be combined into progressively larger groups, tested, and each group used as a tested base to which you can add the remaining items. *Integration testing* usually consists of two aspects: checking each individual interface against its requirements (*conformance testing*), and checking the progress of test transactions through the system as a whole (*end-to-end testing*).

If you've done the system and integration tests in dedicated environments, it's a good idea to re-test the system in the live environment. There may be problems caused by differences in configuration or other software which you should try and detect. Even if you don't have direct access to the live environment (e.g. a PC system for sale to the public) you still need to test in as many representative environments as possible.

How Do I Prepare the Users?

How Should the Users Test the System?

All the testing so far has been from your viewpoint. If the system is intended for specific users, then the system *must* also be tested from their viewpoint. Only they will ultimately be able to judge whether the system works within their business and solves the problems it was intended to. The users cannot delegate this responsibility to you - you must *insist* that they properly accept the system. This is called *user acceptance testing*.

Remind the users that they are not looking for a *perfect* system. They must test against the agreed, documented requirements. It's also a good idea to get them to define the minimum criteria for acceptance.

If the system is a complex one, or if its adoption means changes to the business, then the users should also run trials to simulate the operation of the business using the new system and procedures. They can do this alongside the old system (if one exists), with the results of the two systems being compared: this is a process known as *parallel running*.

Note that this type of testing will require extra resources on the production machine(s): you will probably need to maintain two databases and two sets of user accounts, and the requirements for disk space and memory could be doubled. Even if you're not going to run the old system alongside the new one, you need to plan carefully to make sure that test accounts and data are set up ready for the user tests.

If you have produced a system for sale or more general use, you will not have a specific group of users. However, you should still seek the same sort of feedback from a user's viewpoint. Typically, you will release the product to some potential customers (e.g. users of an older version) and seek their opinions in a programme of *Beta testing*.

How Do We Organise Training?

How will the users be trained? You need to analyse which users perform which tasks, and their current levels of computer literacy, and then decide what training is required for each group. Discuss the options for delivering this training, and the responsibilities for it. Ask the following questions:

? What are realistic prerequisites for each course? Who will ensure they are met?

? Do you need to organise more basic training, in things like keyboard skills, use of the operating system, underlying software or things like the word-processor?

? What is the priority of training given the other duties of trainers and trainees?

? Who will provide the physical resources such as training rooms?

? When will the system be available for training? Is the training system separate from the live system (and, if not, how will training data be kept separate)?

? Who is actually going to do the training? Can external trainers be employed?

? Who will prepare the materials and check that the training works?

You can usefully "test" the training on the users who will do the user testing. Remember that if the users are doing some of the testing, documentation or training, they will need training and support in the appropriate techniques for those tasks, too!

What Else Do I Have To Do?

The other tasks at this stage include the following, but you should discuss the issue widely to see if anyone can identify others:

☞ The users will need intensive support as they begin to use the system, and proper long-term support. You will have to either help set this up, or provide training and documentation for an existing support group.

☞ You may have to help load basic data into the system, or convert existing data.

☞ You may have to either finish off the documentation, or support the users or other groups who are doing so.

☞ The users must have documented procedures which define how the system is used in response to *business* events. You may have to help write these, and should ensure that they make sense in system terms.

☞ You will have to train users how to report and feed back errors and problems.

So How Do I Manage This?

You should have an idea of the way you are going to manage this stage from the very start of the project, and you should put some effort into planning it from the start of the build stage. You need to get a range of resources mobilised, and there are often a number of separate activities on the critical path which you cannot compress. The beginning of the transition stage is *too late* to start planning this exercise.

What is the strategy for implementation? You need to discuss and make a number of key decisions about how you will structure this stage. Take account of practical constraints and the needs of the users, and agree them with all parties. Questions to ask include the following:

? Will you introduce the system on a "big-bang" basis, or will there be a gradual phasing in? Will this phasing be based on a sub-set of system functions, or on sub-groups of users?

? What will happen to existing or manual systems during the introduction? Are there any plans for parallel running? Will this require extra user effort?

? Are the timescales dictated by external events? Can there be adjustment of the plan in response to the actual progress, or are the deadlines absolute?

You may have to be quite cynical when evaluating the answers to these questions. Don't accept, for example, a plan to parallel run the old and new systems together if it's clear that there will be no extra effort available from the users to do so.

Once you've settled the overall structure of the stage, you can draw up a more detailed plan. Just like any other part of your plan, the first thing to do is to make up a list of tasks, and estimate the effort required for each one. It's important to realise that some of these tasks may take a great deal of *dedicated* effort. For example, suppose you are going to test the system, together with the users' procedures, over a weekend. You will need the users and their managers, your team and the support people, system operators, and other players simulating customers and suppliers, for three or four days (including briefings and debriefings). Planning and preparing such an exercise can easily take three or four people a couple of months.

Your plan should include all the various tasks at this stage. The lists on the previous pages are a start, and you should discuss the list of jobs with your colleagues and the users to make sure you haven't missed anything.

Plan *back* from the external deadlines, and *forward* from your own development plans. If these are clearly incompatible (e.g. you should have started training six months ago) then you *must* challenge the deadlines and look for ways of phasing the work. *Don't*, whatever you do, be tempted to quietly drop some of the tasks, or just hush up the problems: if you're not going to make an important deadline then bring that to everyone's attention *now*, not when it's imminent.

Your plan must define the responsibilities, and how they may change. Who will do the work of documentation and training? Who has overall responsibility for implementation? How will the support groups be involved during the early stages, and how will the support structure change during the implementation? You must enumerate precisely the resources which will be provided by your group, the users and others, and when and where they are required.

It's a very good idea to assign an *implementation manager*, who will take overall responsibility for creating and maintaining the implementation plan, and making sure it's acted upon. This person will have to liaise closely with the users and their managers, and it's a good sign of commitment from the users if this person is from the user organisation. On smaller projects you may take this role, and on larger projects the implementation may be treated as a separate project with its own management. These are all fine, as long as someone has clear ownership of the plan, and the job of mobilising the various resources.

If you're creating a system for sale, then you may not have to involve yourself in the users' own testing in the same way. Instead your marketing department or similar will fill the role, and should provide surrogate users for the later stages of testing, trying out the training and so on.

What are the Other Management Challenges?

As project manager, you have two special responsibilities during the transition stage:

✓ Make sure development *stops*. It's very easy for the transition stage to change, almost imperceptibly, into a rolling series of minor changes disguised as bug fixes, with more and more features being added or amended, often without proper funding and approval. When the system delivers the functions in the agreed specification, *stop*, and batch changes for a later phase.

✓ Make sure work is funded and approved. In the implementation plan, you will probably identify tasks you didn't spot before. Make sure, by referring back to the strategies and contracts, you know exactly who is responsible for what, and your work is properly approved.

How Do I Plan for Long-Term Support and Maintenance?

Whether or not you are going to run the long-term support and maintenance for your system, you need to think carefully about how they will be managed, and make sure that the deliverables from the previous stages will meet their requirements.

Consider the internal and external events to which the operators of the system must respond. If they are a separate organisation, ask them - they will have experienced problems which you may not have thought of (or even thought possible!). You need to write procedures to handle each of these events, and you should ideally test them in simulated live running, with suitable simulated problems.

If the eventual operators are separate from your group, they should help write and "own" the procedures, and you must make sure they can maintain them.

The maintainers of the system will use the documentation in two ways: to assess whether a user's request is an error to fix, or a change; and to work out how to fix or change the system. Once the system is updated, they will need to re-test the system, re-deliver it, and make sure the documentation is up-to-date.

Clearly, the easier it is to re-test the system and re-deliver it, the more likely these tasks will be done properly for each batch of changes or fixes. A comprehensive Test Strategy and library of test scripts is a very useful tool to the maintainers. It may be impractical to completely re-test the system at each delivery. Instead, the Test Strategy must indicate which are the most critical aspects of the system (which must be re-tested in all cases). A library of test scripts will allow tests to be targeted at certain functions or parts of the system structure, making the testing at redelivery much more focused.

Proper configuration control, supported by things like build scripts and delivery instructions, will make the process of redelivery quicker and less error-prone.

You shouldn't assume that the maintainers will automatically pick up these techniques and use them without problems. If you have used specific tools for debugging, testing or configuration control, make sure they are available to the maintainers. Make sure that the maintainers have been trained to use the tools, but don't be afraid to provide some documentation or training on the specifics of how they are used on your project.

Equally, don't assume that the maintainers will be as familiar as you with the functions and structure of the system or will have the time to read the documentation to gain that familiarity. In a typical maintenance environment, time will be at a premium. Think about whether you can usefully provide top-level documentation "maps" or checklists, and make sure that in any case you walk through the documentation with the prospective maintainers.

Think about *who* will maintain the documentation you produce, and *how*. The user documentation may be the responsibility of the Implementation Manager or someone in the user organisation. The technical documentation may be maintained by the maintainers, or maybe by some remnant of your project team. Production-related documentation may be maintained by the operators. You will need to make sure that these people have access to the right tools, have been trained to use them, and that the change control process includes updating relevant documentation. It is also a very good idea to plan regular updates of the documentation in the early life of a system. You can be reasonably sure it *will* change, and if your plan allocates time to doing the document maintenance, you are much more likely to do it at a sensible time.

Ask yourself "How maintainable is the code?". Code will often be maintained by the most junior programmers (because the more experienced ones get the more interesting and challenging jobs of new developments or major changes). The code should therefore be as simple and clear as possible. You have to ensure that your programmers avoid questionable or unclear constructs in their code, just as in the documentation. Inspect the code, and check for any potential maintenance problems.

What Are the Potential Problems?

If the maintenance process is not well managed, then a stream of minor amendments will be merged with genuine error corrections to provide rolling changes to the system. If this happens, the documentation may become out of date, and the quality of design and code will be compromised. If a large number of small changes are redelivered separately, then the overhead costs of making the deliveries may add significantly to the costs of maintenance.

You can help to control this by imposing a batched change control process. Make sure that there is a clear procedure for handling error reports and changes, re-testing and redelivering the system, and updating the documentation. If you present this as a *fait accompli* it will be used. If, on the other hand, the maintainers have to create their own procedure, there is no guarantee that all these things will be done.

In the same way, it pays to think of other ways in which your system and procedures can be abused. You can then think of possible preventative measures and build them into the procedures and training you give to the maintainers.

What Are the Risks in the Transition Stage?

Risks may develop during the build or transition stages which will either prevent you delivering on time, or prevent the system being accepted and used by the users. You should consider the possible risks in each category, and take appropriate action to reduce the most severe ones:

☠ Problems with the build and testing may show up as a long list of errors to be fixed, very close to the project deadline. This means late delivery, delivery full of errors, or, in the worst cases, cancellation. The first option is not ideal, but may be acceptable. The second is almost always a recipe for disaster (as is another option, reducing the testing so you don't find out about the bugs at all)! The last means that you have definitely failed, but may be a lower cost option than using and supporting a system of wholly inadequate quality.

Runaway bug lists are either a result of insufficient testing during the build stage (so you find the errors later than necessary), or you find the errors but leave them for correction "later". If you have 500 errors left for correction, then you have no knowledge about the quality of your system, or how near you are to finishing. If, instead, you have already found and cleared 490, and the latest tests have only revealed 10 more errors, then you should be well on the way.

The preventative measure in this case is simple. Do the testing in parallel with the programming, and clear the errors (and retest) before proceeding too far.

☠ The users may request changes, or you make them to "improve" the system. Changes can be caused by a changing technical environment, changes to the users' business, or simply a desire to change the way the system works when the actual implementation does not match the expectations. Whatever the cause, changes can often run away into a protracted, uncontrolled development. You *must* impose rigorous change control, by developing and testing against a known specification, and batching changes for future phases.

☠ The business or the users' priorities may change, which may in turn affect your deadlines or budgets. If this happens, revise your plan and alert the users and managers if you cannot meet the revised constraints. The only real solution is to phase delivery in some way. Just omitting tasks from the implementation plan will cost more and take longer than doing the job properly.

☠ The users may be unwilling or unable to discharge their responsibilities under the implementation plan, possibly because of changes to their business or priorities. Monitor their progress against the plan just like any other contributors to the project, and report any problems to your managers as soon as possible. Don't be tempted to cover up problems: that doesn't help anyone!

- Your users may refuse to accept the system. This is typically for one of three reasons (although they may use other reasons as excuses):

  a. They don't have the time, effort or knowledge to properly perform the acceptance. Trap this early by monitoring against the plan. If necessary, produce a reduced set of key requirements and offer help with preparing (but not running) the tests.

  b. They want a number of changes made to the system. You can accommodate a given, fixed set of changes to the requirements, but they must be properly controlled and the plans modified if necessary. What you cannot do is offer a rolling set of changes with no boundary. You *must* insist that the users agree a definition of the acceptance criteria, at least for this stage.

  c. They claim that the system is not what they expected. If you get this during the transition stage, it's either an excuse covering some fundamental change to the users' plans for the system, or you haven't properly done and communicated the analysis and design. The only preventative measure is lots of formal, regular reviews of the analysis and design documentation.

- Problems of communication can be particularly acute during the transition phase, with a larger number of groups actively involved, and increasing pressure on some or all of them to deliver. You must dedicate some of your time to making sure that communication is full, formal and effective.

- Most of the other risks fall into the general category of "planning problems". They include inadequate physical resources, problems with the machines, infrastructure, or externally supplied components, or tasks forgotten and left out of the implementation plan. You must properly prepare, agree and monitor against this plan just like any other - see the rest of this book!

- If you fail to properly manage this stage, then you may suffer problems of motivation and morale, if, for example, it looks like the system will never be delivered. Your only protection is to *manage properly*, and *communicate*.

Ultimately, accept that some things *will* go wrong, and there *will* be some problems. However, if you follow the approach outlined in the book, by making sure everybody is working to a plan and informed, then you should be able to trap the problems promptly, and find ways to handle them.

How Do I Know When I've Finished?

Ideally, you should develop, test and document all the required functions, the users should accept them (without many changes) and the system should then proceed smoothly into use. While this is the way that all developments *should* end, it's actually quite rare. It tends to be prevented by one of three things: problems with the build or testing, a stream of required changes, or the imposition of deadlines which don't allow you to complete your plan.

You may get to the end of the allocated time or money, and just stop. Alternatively, if the development runs into problems it may be stopped by management decree. You may not deliver anything at all if this happens and your work is still far from completion. Your best protection is the strategy proposed in the previous section.

It's impossible to write bug-free code, and even more difficult to remove all the bugs by testing! Eventually, it is an economic decision (given the required system quality) when to stop testing. If you can, use a statistical measure (such as *mean time between failures*) to specify and verify an acceptable quality. If this is difficult (or inappropriate for a small commercial system) then you must at least classify your errors and check that you have cleared all the most severe ones (and checked for others like them).

You have finished *development* when you have built, tested and documented all the required functions. You will have fixed any errors which prevent the software being used, and trained the users. Bug fixes will then be the work of the maintainers, and any new changes will become part of a new development project. Your aim should be to reach that point as early as practically possible, as otherwise rolling enhancements and changes will destroy your budget and possibly your design.

In order to finish development, you *must* control changes. If the system meets the agreed specification, and a proposed "bug fix" or change means changing *any* existing document, then don't change the system now - batch the idea up as a possible change for a future version instead.

Remember that delivery is not a one-way process. You are always delivering *to* somebody (usually either a user or a tester), and you must understand *who* they are, *what* they are going to do with the delivery and *how* they will decide whether to accept or reject it. You should always try to get formal acceptance (or rejection) of any delivery you make, particularly if it is made against a bug report, action request or change request. If you have formal confirmation that your deliveries have been accepted and all major problems cleared, then you will *know* you have finished the project.

What Do We Deliver?

The following must be delivered from the transition stage. Who delivers what will depend on the division of responsibilities for things like documentation, training and acceptance testing:

▤ *Implementation Plan.* This is the key to this stage, and must contain all the various tasks required to get the system accepted and into use. The implementation manager will use it to manage this stage.

▤ *Working System,* with *updated analysis* and *design documentation.* You *must* keep the technical documentation up-to-date with any changes. It is very easy in the heat of a rush to deliver to forget this, but if you leave it for any length of time, you may find it impossible to catch up! It's much better to develop a habit (which should then become hard to break) of updating the documentation after each change.

▤ *Production-related Documentation.* This will define how the system will fit into the live environment and the various tasks required to support it.

▤ *Regression test scripts.* You must be able to test any new release of the system to check that you have cleared all previously reported errors, and you haven't introduced any new ones.

▤ Completed *User Guide, Training Materials* and *Administrator's Guide.* The latter must include all the procedures for the end users and others to make and restore backups, transfer data in and out of the system, check for proper system operation, and obtain or provide support.

▤ *Service Level Agreements (SLAs).* You should establish a formal agreement between the system's operators, maintainers and users defining things like the target availability of the system, and response times when the users report a problem. This will be very valuable to the manager of the production and maintenance processes (see the next chapter for details).

▤ *Project File,* including *Record of Test Runs and Results,* and log of all *Change* and *Action Requests* and associated correspondence. See page 180 for details.

📖 There are few books which concentrate directly on this stage, but *Software Project Management, How to Write Usable User Documentation, Peopleware* and *The Politics of Projects* may each help in some way.

Production and Maintenance

Once the users have accepted the system and started to use it, there are three main jobs to do: running the system, fixing errors, and making changes. Thus the "production" stage is a mixture of operational work, maintenance, and new developments.

Depending on the structure of your organisation, you may be responsible for some operational tasks, the users may do them themselves, or there may be a specialist "production" group. Whichever is the case, the aim will be to make sure that the users are kept properly informed, they have access when they need it, and their data (and the business processes dependent on it) are properly protected according to documented procedures.

Maintenance is essentially fixing errors in the production system, possibly combined with handling and assessing requests for change. However, it is important to keep the processes of error fixing and making changes separate, as otherwise the changes will tend to be uncontrolled. If you have responsibility for either or both of these processes you will either have to prepare the system for handing over to the maintainers, or create and sustain the right set of attitudes to keep maintenance effective and under control.

Changes should (strictly speaking) go through the whole development life-cycle. In practice, there will usually be an abbreviated version for smaller changes. Every change must be properly evaluated (for cost, including all its impacts, and benefit) and approved. Then, when approved, the documentation must be updated, in the proper order, before the change is made, and the system must be properly re-tested and re-accepted after the change.

How Do I Manage a Maintenance Effort?

If someone else will manage the support and maintenance of your system, you must properly prepare and hand over the system as described in the previous chapter. If you do not, you may find that there is a continuing call on your team and yourself.

If you are going to manage support and/or maintenance, you still need to make these preparations, but they will be for your benefit, not for someone else's. If you are going to maintain another project, currently being developed, then you have a checklist of the deliverables and support you should expect from that project team.

However, you may have to support an existing *legacy* system. It may not have the supporting documentation, or that may be out of date. The design may be obscure, or the code clumsy. There may be a case for replacing the system, but it is not always (or even often) economically possible to do so. However, you should make sure that this evaluation is based on the *real* costs of maintenance and changes.

If there is no short-term prospect of replacing the system, you need to think what can be done to replace the missing deliverables. There are various options, depending on what work you need to do. If you are mainly fixing errors or need to improve performance, then *restructuring* the code into a more modular format (and maybe using a more modern variant of the language) may help. If you have to make some changes, then you can *re-engineer* and gradually tidy up the system. If your ultimate goal is to replace the system, then you can even *reverse engineer* a specification from the existing system. Whichever option you take, you should reverse engineer a set of regression tests and configuration descriptions so that you can ensure the continuity of the old system as you change it. Don't assume that just because the documents don't exist now, that you have to manage without them forever.

Whether or not your system is properly prepared for maintenance, you have to establish a few key agreements defining how you will manage the process. The main document is a *Service Level Agreement* with the users, which must include:

⊙ Targets for the availability of the system and support, the time you will take to respond to a reported error, and the time you will take to process a change request. If you feel confident of your ability to fix errors, then you may also agree a *mean time to repair* (MTTR) - the time from a reported error to its fix being delivered.

Don't over-commit yourself. Be conservative with your estimates, and quote these targets as "averages" or "for 90% of cases", to allow for the occasions when you won't meet them.

⊙ The procedures for reporting, classifying and handling a reported problem. The procedure for evaluating and approving a change, and agreeing a cost and delivery date.

The Service Level Agreement should be backed up by a budget for maintenance work. Otherwise, you will have to separately agree a cost for each fix, which can be very clumsy. The maintenance budget might even cover small changes. However, even if you have a budget you will still have to regularly report to the users and your managers what work you have done and how the budget is being used. Alternatively, you may be able to get the users to control the budget, and assign priorities to their requests based on their consumption of it.

It is important to collect information about each problem or change request you tackle. This information should include the time to respond to the request, and the time to deliver a fix or change evaluation. It should include your assessment of the severity of the problem, and a record of which item(s) were faulty. If you do not collect such data, you cannot prove whether or not you are meeting your targets under the SLA. Even if you don't have the constraint of a formal SLA and budget, you should still collect this information, to justify the maintenance effort to management inspection.

Agree a system of classification for problems. Keep it simple: a two-level system may be adequate, and you can simply ask the question "does this stop you working?". If the answer is "yes", it's urgent, otherwise it's non-urgent. You must also distinguish between errors and changes.

A maintenance effort has its own special management problems. You must ensure that your resources (both human and physical) are adequate for the task, and demand better resources (or training) if they are not. You have to make sure that procedures are followed, so that the quality of the system is maintained and ideally improved. Morale can be poor, particularly if you are patching up a system of indifferent quality. You may then find that the challenge of personal responsibility for part of a system, or the visible improvements to quality from a re-engineering exercise can pay handsome dividends in terms of the ability of your team to perform their tasks.

📖 *Decline and Fall of the American Programmer* has a very good chapter on reverse engineering and its variants. *Software Project Management* deals in some detail with the problems of maintenance and how to tackle them.

What Are the Right Attitudes to Maintenance?

Successful maintenance is all about attitude. Once you've got a reasonable management framework, with the right resources, it's largely a question of the right approach and self-discipline. Many of the comments in this section apply equally to the other stages of development, but they're particularly important during maintenance, when it's very easy to lose control of changes and your budget.

It's never easy to decide what is a "bug fix" and what is a small change. However, it's important to do so - otherwise, you risk two things: causing problems to other users or systems because something changes without warning, and providing functions which are not properly justified and approved.

> If the documentation's right and the system's wrong, it's an error. If **any** documentation has to change, then it's a change.

The simple solution is to adopt the rule above. Assume that the documentation describes what the system *should* do (after all, that's what it's supposed to be there for). If the documentation describes something and it doesn't work that way, then you can fix the error so that the system matches the documentation. Just remember to point this out when you redeliver the system - someone may have been relying on "wrong" behaviour!

However, if as a result of doing what a user requests, or of fixing obviously wrong behaviour, you will have to update *any* documentation, then treat it as a change. This will have to be formally proposed, its impact, cost and benefit evaluated, and formal approval given. Obviously, this means that for *all* actions you take you *must* check the state of the documentation - you have to positively confirm that the documentation is correct even if you're fixing a bug.

Don't implement (or add) unnecessary features, just because they're "easy", or the competition has them. They all have a cost in bugs (you can't write error-free code) and increased complexity as well as time and effort. Be prepared to ask "will the system fail to meet requirements if we *don't* do this". If an extra feature you have suggested will really deliver a benefit, then don't be afraid to offer it up as a formally requested change for proper evaluation and approval. On the other hand, if you or your programmers can't be bothered to do this, then the feature clearly isn't worth implementing.

Beware of the dangers of flexibility. Highly flexible functions, tools or applications may provide more ways of working, but they also provide much greater scope for mistakes, and they're much harder to test and debug. Resist the temptation to build one "mega" function if two small, targeted ones will do instead.

There's no such thing as a "simple" change: all changes (even cosmetic ones) need retesting. *Don't* "clean up" the code, unless you know you can retest it. You may sometimes spot opportunities to avoid or remove duplication, find a simpler solution or address known design weaknesses (refactoring) – this is a good thing, but you must make the changes, reintegrate and retest in a controlled way.

> If it ain't broke, don't fix it

Do try to create a positive attitude to fixing problems and checking they're fixed. Don't accept "I couldn't see anything wrong" or "I couldn't reproduce the problem" - bugs don't just go away. If either of these are the case then check that the users are using the version of the software you think they are - there may be a failure of configuration control. *Do* create a list of all reported errors to be positively "signed off" by the assigned investigator, fixer, re-tester and, eventually, the user.

If you come up against a seemingly intractable problem, there's a great temptation to canvass ideas from your colleagues, and to "try" more and more arcane solutions, essentially hacking the code in an attempt to find something that "works". It's much better to do two things: *think*, and *read the manual*. You'll be surprised how often there's a proper, maintainable solution to your problem.

If you have a number of related or similar errors, check that you are tackling the root-cause problem, and not the symptom. If, for example, a certain routine can fail it's much better to rewrite it rather than coding error traps into six places which call it!

Get into the habit of fixing bugs before implementing new features. Write, test and fix in small cycles if you are writing new software. The benefits are better knowledge of the status of the system, a chance to prevent similar errors, and better morale. It's much better to have tested and fixed 60% of your system than to have *written* 100% and *completed* 0%.

Remember, the job of fixing a bug or implementing a small change isn't complete until the documentation has been updated and the tests re-run. Don't allow changes to be delivered without this: you could make good documentation useless, and cause great problems for the users and testers.

> The job isn't complete till the paperwork's done!

📖 *Writing Solid Code* contains some very sound advice (with a lot more detail than here) on attitudes to writing, fixing and changing software.

What Happens When Someone Important Leaves?

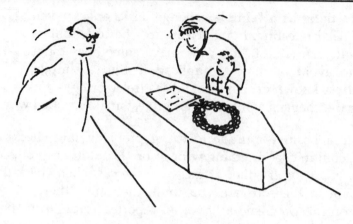

*"I realise this may be an awkward time,
but do you recall him ever mentioning 'source code'?"*

People will leave your project in one of three ways. They will depart naturally at the end of the project or stage, or following a defined notice period if they move to another job. These are types of departure for which you can plan and prepare. As the cartoon implies, the other class of departure is the unplanned one - it's not so common, and not necessarily permanent (e.g. in the case of sickness), but it's a risk you need to acknowledge and allow for.

In all cases, your best protection is a policy of "document first". If a person has documented what he was going to do, then you can pick up more or less where he left off. If you just have a mass of undocumented code, the only approach may be to throw it away and start again!

If you can afford it, make sure that two people understand the key aspects of the requirements and design. This isn't wasted effort: if, for example, the senior designer walks through all his documentation with another team member, then you are getting a review and some training, which has value in its own right.

Think about who might be able to "shadow" each member of your team. You might be able to switch roles within the team, or know another member of the organisation, or a freelance worker, with similar abilities. If the worst comes to the worst, it's much better to be able to ask for X, rather than having to start recruitment from square one just at the worst time. In any case, you may need to arrange cover for holidays and so forth - if there is a nominated second then this sort of planning is much easier.

Don't forget to include yourself in these plans! You and I both know that you're not going to leave the company or walk under a bus, but have you thought about jury service, or what would happen if you won the lottery? The best way to create a professional approach across your team is to demonstrate through your own actions that the professional thing to do is to plan for the worst.

At any time, and for each member of the team, you should be able to:

☑ Say exactly what they are working on, down to the individual module, error report, change request or document,

☑ Find out how far they have got through the job,

☑ Find a document which describes what they have to do next,

☑ Identify the tools and specific technical skills which that person is using,

☑ Find and take control of the work in progress - this includes getting access to accounts and private directories (in accordance with the security rules of your organisation), and checking work in and out of code or document control systems,

☑ Name another member of the organisation who is shadowing the work and can either pick it up, or brief you on it.

In the case of a planned departure, you should use the above list, or an extended variant of it, to debrief the leaver. Resist the temptation to get a good programmer to do lots of new code or significant changes just before he leaves. It's of much more value to you to make sure that the work which he has already done is properly documented, tested and handed over. Work which has been coded but not properly completed is of very little value, and you may end up throwing some or all of it away. Instead, as soon as you know about the departure, create a formal plan listing the handover tasks and when he will do them.

Not all departures are as dramatic as in the cartoon, but they are all capable of ruining your careful plans. Only by planning for the unexpected will you be able to deal with it!

How Do Systems Die?

The old adage (right) is not really true. Sudden death is rare, but there are a number of ways a system can die, with dramatically different implications for the project's fate and chance of ressurection:

Old systems never die they just fade away.

- *The living dead: a failed system.* A failed project can be cancelled before it ever gets into production. However - beware! Like a vampire, a failed system has a nasty habit of rising from the dead and sucking the organisation's life-blood (its time and money resources), no matter how many times you drive a stake through its heart. There's always a temptation to try and salvage something, but if a system has failed because of some basic flaws in analysis, design or execution it is probably unwise to try to revive it.

- *Death in obscurity: the users don't or won't use the system.* There can be many reasons for this: fundamental errors in analysis, poor implementation, and changes to the users' business among them. If the users feel they have a system forced onto them, without proper consultation, they may just ignore it, and only very strong management directives may change it. This type of death is rarely planned, and the system may just become ignored over time, although still nominally in production. This tends to be a lingering death, but the system may be revived by some modifications, or by strong management action.

- *Senility: the system gradually deteriorates during maintenance.* It is very difficult to maintain absolute control of a system as you maintain it for a period of years. It may become progressively more difficult to add new features, or to support new ways of working. Eventually the system must be replaced.

- *Retirement: the honourable way.* The available technology (and with it the users' expectations), or the business changes and the old system, once adequate, needs to be retired. It can be fairly easy to plan its replacement, but be careful to manage the users' expectations. There's no guarantee that a new system will be faster or better, particularly if it's much cheaper or more functional. Watch out for implicit requirements ("the old system could do this...") which don't find their way into the documentation. Don't make assumptions about how the old functions are actually used in practice, or the learning curve for new ones, and don't underestimate the natural resistance to change. Otherwise it's just like any other development - good luck!

Success!

Successfully completing a
system which others then use is
a very rewarding experience.
It's even better if you can bring
the project in on time and
within budget. All this can be
yours if you follow the
principles in this book, and add
to them from your experience,
and the ideas of your colleagues
and other books.

At any time, you can check you are
on the right lines. Ask yourself the following:

☑   Have I got an up-to-date plan? Does it answer, clearly, *what? why? when? where? how?* and *who?*

☑   Have I *communicated* the plan to my team, the users and my managers?

☑   Am I *using* the plan? Do I know how far each task has progressed against it?

☑   Are we following the procedures and standards we agreed? Have I *checked*?

☑   Have we thought about the risks? Have I *planned* to prevent or handle them?

☑   Do we have a clear specification for the system?

If you can answer "yes" to these, you're probably on the right track. It won't *guarantee* success, but your prospects are very good! If you have to answer "no", then you know where to concentrate your efforts.

Good luck!

Further Reading

This book is only an introduction, and you'll probably want to read more on many of the topics. The following books provide further information in a number of key areas. It isn't meant to be a complete bibliography, but is instead a list of books which I have found to be relevant to software development as described in the rest of this book.

I have focused on books which are short, well-written, focussed and entertaining or inspiring. There aren't many technology books here, because technology changes faster than I can update this book. You can always find more detailed, technical and up-to-date reviews and reading lists at my website, *www.andrewj.com*

The comments that follow the basic details of each book are mine alone, and I hope the authors will forgive me if their intention was different from what I observe!

Software - General

Software Shock, the Danger and the Opportunity, by **Roger S. Pressman** and **S. Russell Herron**, Dorset House. This is the book to read if you're new to the world of software and its problems. It explains in very simple terms what software is, how we create it, and what the problems are with those processes.

The Soul of a New Machine, by **Tracy Kidder**, Black Bay Books 2000. This is the very readable true story of the team who created a new computer, and the technology and man-management problems which had to be overcome. It gives a very useful insight into the psychology of "computer people".

Why Does Software Cost So Much?, by **Tom DeMarco**, Dorset House 1995. DeMarco presents a series of essays on software, software processes, and how the world of IT and high technology sometimes fails to match the expectations of users and business.

Man- and Project Management

Peopleware - Productive Projects and Teams, by **Tom DeMarco** and **Timothy Lister**, Dorset House 1987. This exceptional book explains how to get the best (or the worst!) from the people who are your key development resource, with good practices for building and managing productive teams. It's very readable. DeMarco & Lister also do occasional public courses based on the same material, which I can wholeheartedly recommend.

Debugging the Development Process, by **Steve Maguire**, Microsoft Press 1994. Following on from *Writing Solid Code,* this looks at a range of management issues in typical software development processes, and presents advice based on practical experience at Microsoft.

The Mythical Man-Month, by **Frederick P. Brooks, Jr.,** Addison-Wesley 1975 & 1995. This is the classic text on software project management. The technology is rather out of date now, but the ideas on team structure are still fine, and it's still one of the best basic texts on the importance of a well-structured design.

AntiPatterns, by **William J. Brown, Raphael C. Malveau, Hays W. "Skip" McCormick III** and **Thomas J. Mowbray**, Wiley 1998. Antipatterns are the opposite of patterns – common ways in which things can go wrong. This often-amusing book identifies a number of common AntiPatterns in development processes, architecture and management, and offers some suggestions on how they can be addressed. If you think you're failing, and you're not sure why, this is a good place to start.

The Politics of Projects, by **Robert Block**, Ashgate Publishing Group 1983. Explains the political and "people" problems which cause developments to fail, and how to read the politics of a management situation and exploit it to maximise your chances of success.

Principles of Software Engineering Management, by **Tom Gilb**, Addison-Wesley 1988. A great book full of ideas, in particular how to structure a development into phases and what to deliver when. Very good on risk management, project structure and estimating. The terminology and details of some methods are a bit clumsy, particularly in the latter part of the book, so it does need to be "interpreted" to fit in with your own development methods.

Controlling Software Projects, by **Tom DeMarco**, Prentice Hall 1982. This book concentrates on methods of measuring and estimating software development. If you want to get really good at estimating in an organisation that will do a number of similar developments, then this book is essential.

Making it Happen, by **John Harvey-Jones**, Fontana 1988. Not really about software, but an excellent text on the problems of man management from someone who's proven he knows how to do it properly!

Make It So, by **Wess Roberts Ph.D.** and **Bill Ross**, Pocket Books 1995. Put into the words of Captain Jean-Luc Picard, and illustrated with incidents from episodes of *Star*

Trek - the Next Generation, this is a series of essays on common management issues and how to tackle them. It's amusing, especially if you're a Trekkie, but the management advice is sound and valuable.

Wicked Problems, Righteous Solutions, by **Peter DeGrace** and **Leslie Hulet Stahl**, Prentice Hall 1990. This book looks at various project structures and development methods, and explains their strengths and weaknesses. In particular it looks at those classes of problem which will *not* be satisfactorily analysed by traditional methods, and proposes alternative ways to their resolution.

Decline and Fall of the American Programmer, by **Edward Yourdon**, Prentice Hall 1993. A book which tries to explain why the typical programmer (and project) is not adopting those methods which would make life easier, and what the results may be. It includes a clear explanation of steps the author believes must be taken by software producers to remain competitive.

Rise & Resurrection of the American Programmer, by **Edward Yourdon**, Prentice Hall 1996. A follow-up to the previous book, this is more up-beat. It describes how the software development business continued to thrive through the 1990s, and the practices that enabled it to do so.

Death March, by **Edward Yourdon**, Prentice Hall 1997. Some software projects, usually larger ones, become "mission impossible" projects, and seem doomed to failure even despite enormous efforts from all involved. Yourdon describes this phenomenon, and then offers some practical advice on how to avoid or address it.

Software Project Management – A Practitioner's Approach, by **E. M. Benettan**, McGraw Hill 1992. An excellent book with a similar scope to this one, although the style is quite different being targeted at more senior managers. It's very good on formal and "public domain" standards, and on structured methods of estimation, but is not so strong on things like design and testing, being a bit prescriptive rather than explaining why some approaches are advised.

The Secrets of Consulting – A Guide to Giving & Getting Advice Successfully, by **Gerald M. Weinberg**, Dorset House 1985. Not only for consultants, this is full of excellent advice for anyone who wants to identify problems, propose solutions or make changes in any sort of business.

Software Project Survival Guide, by **Steve McConnell**, Microsoft 1998. This is a very helpful book with a similar scope to this one, providing practical advice for each stage in software development.

Analysis and Methods

UML Distilled, by **Martin Fowler**, Addison Wesley 1997. A concise and very readable introduction to the Unified Modelling Language, this also describes a number of techniques for using it effectively.

The Rational Unified Process, by Philippe Krutchen, Addison Wesley 1998. This is a companion book to *UML Distilled*, describing a method for developing component-based software using UML. This is a short book which focuses on the principles and how to structure work using RUP.

Writing Effective Use Cases, by **Alistair Cockburn**, Addison Wesley 2001. Use Cases are the key to requirements analysis in many modern methods, especially those based on UML. This book discusses standards for Use Case modelling and construction, and presents ways to tackle a range of common problems.

Mastering the Requirements Process, by **Suzanne Robertson** and **James Robertson**, Addison Wesley 1999. An excellent guide to analysis processes, and how to find, explore, evaluate and manage the requirements for a system.

Business Modeling with UML – Business Patterns at Work, **Hans-Erik Eriksson** and **Magnus Penker**, Wiley 2000. This is an excellent description of to how to use UML to model businesses, their goals and processes. A large part of the book is given over to a number of very useful patterns for business analysis, but it's also strong on the principles, and how to use some more complex parts of UML, like the Object Constraint Language.

Realizing e-Business with Components, by **Paul Allen**, Addison Wesley 2001. This book does much more than it says on the cover. As well how to use components in e-Business solutions, it also describes the complete process of analysing and designing hybrid systems (combinations of legacy software and new components) using UML, with lots of examples. It comprehensively discusses the processes and management issues of component-based development.

Enterprise Modeling with UML – Designing Successful Software through Business Analysis, **Chris Marshall**, Addison Wesley 2000. This book tells you how to extend the use of UML to model big systems and high-level business problems. It's very strong on class modelling, but less comprehensive than *Business Modeling with UML*.

The Unified Modeling Language Reference Manual, **James Rumbaugh**, **Ivar Jacobson** and **Grady Booch**, Addison Wesley 1999. The definitive guide to UML, written by the three men credited with creating it, is a good reference work, although other books are better for specific aspects.

Introducing SSADM Version 4, by **G Longworth**, NCC Blackwell 1992. SSADM is a method used throughout the British public sector, and on many private sector projects. This book is a very clear and commendably brief introduction to the method, and to its main analysis techniques.

CASE*Method Entity Relationship Modelling, by **Richard Barker**, Oracle 1989. This is a very good and comprehensive but readable text on data analysis using ERDs.

Agile Modeling, by **Scott W. Ambler**, Wiley 2002. Extending the idea of agile development from coding into modelling, this brings rapid application development principles together with the use of effective analysis and design techniques. It's a very good guide if you're trying to decide how much modelling is necessary and sufficient.

Extreme Programming Explained, by **Kent Beck**, Addison Wesley 2000. Extreme Programming is one of the most radical Rapid Application Development methods. I'm not a full supporter of XP, as I fear it generates fragile designs which are difficult to change and integrate. However many of the concepts, like pair programming, can also be of great value in more formal methods, and they are well described here.

Software Architecture – Organizational Principles and Patterns, by **David M. Dikel**, **David Kane** and **James R. Wilson**, Prentice Hall 2001. This is a book about how to make changes across an organisation. Its focus is software architecture, but the advice is equally valuable to anyone trying to sell ideas, or who needs to understand how success is dictated by people and processes, not technology.

Architecture and Design

Refactoring – Improving the Design of Existing Code, by **Martin Fowler**, Addison Wesley 2000. Setting out from the assertion that many designs are poor, and most can be improved, this describes how to improve common design flaws, and how to manage the process of making changes to existing systems.

Expressive Systems – A manifesto for radical business software, by **Richard Pawson**, CSC 2000. One of the most influential recent books on design, this explains why we should be building software which helps users tackle problems instead of just automating predefined business processes. This means making the objects within a system much more visible to the user. It *is* radical, and doesn't sit easily with the popularity of crude web-based interfaces, but it may change how you think software should work. I'm proud to be a contributor.

About Face – the Essentials of User Interface Design, by **Alan Cooper**, IDG Books 1995. This is probably the best book on traditional user interface design – how to design business and consumer software using common real-world platforms so that it does what the user wants.

Tog on Software Design, by **Bruce Tognazzini**, Addison Wesley 1996. Slightly less "real world" than *About Face*, this provides an insight into where computer systems might be going and how we should be interacting with them, but then also includes a great deal of practical advice on how software should behave to make it truly usable.

The Human Factor – Designing Computer Systems for PEOPLE, by **Richard Rubinstein** and **Harry Hersh**, Prentice Hall 1991. A very readable book on what's wrong with most human-computer interfaces, and some sound ideas on how to get it right.

UML Components, by **John Cheesman** and **John Daniels**, Addison Wesley 2001. A very influential book, this provides a guide to effectively using UML to model and define component-based systems.

The Windows Interface Guidelines for Software Design, Microsoft Press 1995. This defines the standard for user-computer interfaces on which much modern application software has been built, outlining a common set of principles which should form the basis of any modern software's design.

Enterprise Application Integration, by **David S. Linthicum**, Addison Wesley 2000. This is a good if occasionally repetitive introduction to the various ways systems can be integrated together. Unfortunately the original edition predates the popularity of web services, but it's still probably the best summary of other techniques.

How Buildings Learn, by **Stewart Brand**, Penguin 1994. Successful buildings have to be built to last, but have to adapt to the changing needs of their occupants over time. Brand's book studies the ways in which that process can succeed or fail. Many of his findings have direct analogies in the flexibility and durability of software, and this is essential reading for anyone trying to build flexible, long-lived systems.

The Art of the Long View, by **Peter Schwartz**, Wiley 1991, 1996. Planning businesses and their IT systems requires being able to see into the future. Schwartz can't guarantee that, but he offers the technique of scenario analysis, by which you can explore what *might* happen, and decide what you need to do to allow for it.

IT Architectures and Middleware, by **Chris Britton**, Addison Wesley 2000. This book does two things – it's a very good overview of different IT architectures and their characteristics, and the latter part of the book is an excellent guide to making large, complex systems scalable, reliable and secure.

Pattern-Oriented Software Architecture – A System of Patterns, by **Frank Buschmann, Regine Meunier, Hans Rohnert, Peter Sommerlad** and **Michael Stal**, Wiley 1996. This is a very good specialist "patterns" book, focussing on common patterns for architecture and high-level design.

Database Design for Smarties – Using UML for Data Modeling, by **Robert J. Muller**, Morgan Kaufman 1999. This is a very comprehensive guide to all aspects of data modelling and database design, particularly useful because it is UML based.

The Software Architect's Profession, by **Marc Sewell** and **Laura Sewell**, Prentice-Hall 2001. This book explains exactly what software architects do, how they behave, and how the profession is developing.

Coding and Configuration Control

Writing Solid Code, by **Steve Maguire**, Microsoft Press 1993. One of the few books which concentrates on the responsibilities of the programmer: to produce high-quality, *tested* code which traps errors at creation, rather than leaving them for later detection and correction. Although it concentrates on 'C', most of the techniques can be applied to any programming language.

Code Complete, by **Steve McConnell**, Microsoft 1993. The aim of this book, as the title suggests, is to form a reference on both good coding practice and how to solve common coding problems. Although some aspects are now a little out of date, the core guides to good practice and algorithm descriptions are still valuable.

Software Configuration Management, by **Wayne A. Babich**, Addison-Wesley 1986. This is one of the few books to concentrate on this key aspect of software development. It's strong on the principles, including ideas like information hiding and clean interfaces as a way to ease the configuration control task, and extends to a practical discussion of tools such as *SCCS* within Unix.

Testing and Quality Assurance

The Tester's Handbook, by **Geoff Quentin**, QCC Ltd. 1992. A very readable little book which explains the principles and a number of key techniques in testing. It doesn't go into great detail on any of the methods, but does provide enough practical guidance to get started.

The Art of Software Testing, by **Glenford J. Myers**, Wiley 1979. A first-class discussion of the principles of good testing. However, the detailed methods don't really take account of the complexity of larger systems, and don't extend to more modern software structures such as those based on object-oriented or event-driven principles.

The Complete Guide to Software Testing, by **Bill Hetzel**, QED 1988. An overview of practical test methods and tools, and a discussion of the related management issues.

Software Inspection: An Effective Method for Software Project Management, by **Dorothy Graham** and **Tom Gilb**, Addison-Wesley 1993. A practical guide to using software inspections to cut development time, and increase productivity and quality.

Jurassic Park, by **Michael Crichton**, Arrow 1991. Although never intended as a textbook, this story includes possibly the best discussion I have read of dramatic systems failure, and the danger (literally!) of not properly testing your exception conditions.

Documentation and Communication

How to Write Usable User Documentation, by **Edmond H. Weiss**, Oryx Press 1991. This is an excellent book on how to write effective and compact documentation of any sort, although it concentrates on user documentation. I have used a lot of the ideas (e.g. a fixed-length modular format) in writing my book.

The Economist Style Guide, Economist Books Ltd. 1991. This book was originally developed as a guide for people writing for *The Economist* magazine. It contains a compact, readable guide to good writing style, a comprehensive guide to good use of English (in both British and American contexts), and also a very interesting (but perhaps less relevant) fact checker for writers of political or economic articles.

So, What's Your Point?, by **James C. Wetherbe** and **Bond Wetherbe**, Mead Publishing 1996. A very readable guide to the problems of oral communication, and how to explain yourself and negotiate to get what you want without hurting people's feelings. If you feel that discussions and debates are always a battle, then this is the book for you.

Index

WWW.WWISA.ORG

The Worldwide Institute of Software Architects (WWISA) is a non-profit professional organization dedicated to the establishment of a formal profession of software architecture and to provide information and services to software architects and their clients - analogous to the formation of the American Institute of Architects roughly 140 years ago. The essential tenet of WWISA is that there is a perfect analogy between building and software architecture and the classical role of the architect needs to be introduced into the software construction industry.

The architect, whether designing structures of brick or computer code, forms the bridge between the world of the client and that of the technical builders. This critical bridge has been missing from the software industry resulting in the decades-long software crisis. Entire software structures are dysfunctional or have been scrapped entirely - before seeing a single "inhabitant." We have simply been building huge, complex structures without architects, without blueprints.

WWISA was established in 1998 and now has over 2,000 members in 64 countries. Membership is open to practicing and aspiring software architects, professors, students, CIO's and CEO's. Members participate to promote training and degree programs, develop architectural standards and guiding principles, and work toward a standard body of shared knowledge. We are client advocates; they are our driving force. We hope to become the clients' bridge to successful software construction by leveraging the full range of technology in their favor.